8:28

HOPE IN THE DARKNESS

ISBN: (e-book) 979-8-89283-026-3
ISBN: (Paperback) 978-1-962071-45-1
ISBN: (Hardcover) 978-1-962071-47-5
Library of Congress Control Number: TXu 2-188-469 (2020)

Graphic Designer: Denise Sullivan
Book Interior Design: Books to Hook Publishing, LLC.
Publisher: 8:28 Hope Publishing - Books to Hook Publishing, LLC.

Editing Acknowledgements:
Barry Brinker, Julie DeMarco, Rechelle Conde Nau,
Brian Thompson, Kara Errico, Sana Abuleil and Marie B.

www.828HOPE.com

First printing edition 2024.

"Karen Hacker has written a beautiful book of comfort and support to anyone grieving the loss of a loved one. She knows deep loss personally, and shares the hope that sustained her as she walked through very dark days of anguish and confusion. What I admire most about Karen is her decision to channel her loss and love into the hundreds of hurting couples whom she has served through the Empty Arms support group at Saddleback Church. Read this book and pass it on to a griever."

Kay Warren
Co-Founder Saddleback Church | Author | Speaker | Advocate

"As a person who has been working in the field of loss for the past 25 years, I am often called upon by friends and family for advice on what to do for someone who has experienced a significant loss. I used to suggest several different resources but I am so grateful now to have a single resource that I can share that covers everything that's important all in one place. Karen's practical experience and godly approach to some of life's toughest questions makes this a book that I will be handing out to everyone I care about and love."

Marcella Johnson
Founder of the Comfort Cub

"Karen Hacker has served in the Ministry of Empty Arms at Saddleback Church for almost 30 years. She has written 8:28 Hope in the Darkness based on her experience in that ministry and gives practical tools to give hope to the hurting. Most importantly, Karen shares insights learned from her own personal journey through grief and loss. I will definitely be recommending this book!"

Cheryl Baker
Co-founder of Celebrate Recovery | Co-founder of Grief's Healing Choices

"As a licensed therapist, I have the privilege of working with individuals, couples, and families in times of extreme darkness. One of the hardest things for any client to navigate in session, usually surrounds the concept of grief and loss. The author of this book has skillfully navigated a very difficult topic through the use of her own experiences with loss, the use of wellness-based activities, her faith, along with proven Psychological modalities and strategies. I would highly recommend this book to anyone struggling with loss and I will personally be using this book with clients as a means of recapturing peace and a hope for the future."

Brian Thompson MA, LMFT, CATC-IV, CI, CHt, CCT
Licensed Marriage & Family Therapist #104710

"Inspiring and heartfelt, 8:28 Hope in the Darkness is a beautiful resource for those suffering a loss. Through her own journey, Karen provides a way to inspire hope in the darkness of grief. Sharing raw emotion and resilience, she guides readers toward purposeful living amid grief. A must-read for anyone seeking comfort and understanding through the difficulties of life."

Lori Moore, RN
Sharp HospiceCare, 11th hour volunteer | Sharp Memorial Board of Trustees, Chair | Sharp Moore MountainView Hospice Home, Poway, CA

"Karen has been a light for so many over the years. It isn't possible to endure the loss she has experienced without her faith. She understands what people need when they are in a dark place. They don't need toxic positivity; they need connection, understanding and someone who will listen. And they need someone who believes they can find light again. Karen is that person."

Veronica Valli
Recovery Coach | Award-winning Author of Soberful | Podcaster: Soberful

"As a pastor and friend, I love Karen and Rick Hacker for the ways they have faced the greatest pain with trust in Jesus, and then out of that pain began to minister to others. They are one of the greatest examples I know of the truth that our greatest ministry comes out of our greatest pain. This book is just the latest expression of that heart to serve. Again and again they have taught those who have the empty arms of loss to throw themselves into the loving arms of Jesus. This is a book that will help you to find God's grace, love and strength in the midst of your grief."

Tom

Tom Holladay
Saddleback Church | Purpose Driven Training | P.E.A.C.E Plan | DrivetimeDevotions.com

"In her book, Karen takes the reader through her heartbreaking story of loss — more tragedy than any one human should have to endure. We follow as she navigates her journey with gut-wrenching honesty, always seeking God's compassionate healing and guidance as she provides comfort to her readers.

I am so grateful for her courage to be transparent and her willingness to be used by God. I am also incredibly confident that anyone who reads *8:28 Hope in the Darkness* will find solace, hope and healing in her words."

Shari Bridgman, PhD
Licensed Psychotherapist
Founder, **Empty Arms Support Group**, Saddleback Church
Author, *In Heavenly Arms: Grieving the Loss and Healing the Wounds of Miscarriage*

"If you are feeling loss, and wondering how on earth God uses it for your good, look no further than *8:28 Hope in the Darkness*. You will be able to trace the hand of God in your grief and find the encouragement you need to endure well."

Rechelle Conde Nau
Postcaster: Unabashed You | Author of Standing Tall – A Collecton of Mourning

"Karen is a light and inspiration to families who have experienced pregnancy or infant loss. For many years, she has been dedicated to helping families navigate grief. This book is another beautiful example of her giving back to the loss community and sharing her compassion, understanding and journey after losing her first two babies, and then suddenly losing seven immediate family members."

Kristyn Von Rotz
Founder of Forever Footprints | Founder OC Walk to Remember

"If you've experienced the loss of a baby due to miscarriage, stillbirth, or infant loss, then I recommend reading 8:28 Hope in the Darkness. Karen Hacker vulnerably shares her story of losing her first son. Through her personal testimony and her acronym for Hope in the Darkness, you will walk away with Biblical truth and practical tools to help you through your grief. In addition, she shares the profound grief she experienced due to the successive losses of her sister, mother, brother, father, and in-laws in a brief span of time. This book will help anyone who has lost a loved one, no matter the age."

Jodi Rosser
Author of *Depth: Growing Through Heartbreak to Strength* / Podcaster - Depth

"Karen Hacker has written an inspiring book that helps the reader find light in the darkness of grief. Karen knows firsthand about grief having lost two babies and seven immediate family members within five years. She shares how she was able to turn her pain into purpose by trusting God to bring good out of her tragedy. She understands the grief process and has used her experience to help others on their grief journey. Karen reminds us that endings lead to new beginnings. She provides a hope-filled book that will deepen your faith in the nature of God and his ability to bring good out of seemingly unmanageable situations. I highly recommend it!"

Dr. Dave Page, DMIN, MBA, MDIV
Pastor//Grief Educator//Speaker/Author of The School of Grief: A Guide to Finding Hope, Meaning and Purpose After Loss.

"As a Psychotherapist, I can share first-hand, majority of my clients are seeking therapy for support in dealing with grief of some kind in their life. Supporting clients where they are is important; helping clients work through the steps of grief is part of the healing journey, along with finding ways to honor our loved ones are just as important! The book describes the different emotions one faces and how to move forward, plus describes ways to honor our loved ones! This book will be a great "tool in the toolbox" for clients to have!"

Jozlyn Torres, MSHR, MA, AMFT, EMDR
Associate Marriage Family Therapist #129628

"As one walks the path of grief, having those who understand is critical. Karen and Rick have experienced tragic loss and are making it through—these are the critical ones. Karen has been in that dark place of loss and has made the intentional choice of helping others, even when she wrestles herself. It's a sacred trust. This book sheds light on the journey, calls out the difficulties, and answers the "why me" questions. This is a must-guide for anyone dealing with loss and death."

Pastor Jim Dobbs
Grief Care Pastor at Saddleback Church

8:28

HOPE IN THE DARKNESS

A Pathway from Heartbreak to Healing and Hope

KAREN BADAL HACKER

FORWARD

I met Karen and Rick Hacker many years ago during my own struggle with infertility and prenatal grief. Although my journey was devastatingly painful, it was the genesis for the **Empty Arms Support Group** at Saddleback Church and my book: *In Heavenly Arms*. It was through Empty Arms that I first had the opportunity to become acquainted with Karen and Rick Hacker.

Shortly after participating in the support group, the Hackers stepped up to serve as leaders of the ministry. Twenty-eight years later, they are still serving with selfless dedication and deep, abiding empathy born of their own grief journey.

In her book, Karen takes the reader through her heartbreaking story of loss — more tragedy than any one human should have to endure. We follow as she navigates her journey with gut-wrenching honesty, always seeking God's compassionate healing and guidance as she provides comfort to her readers.

I am so grateful for her courage to be transparent and her willingness to be used by God. I am also incredibly confident that anyone who reads *8:28 Hope in the Darkness* will find solace, hope, and healing in her words.

Shari Bridgman, PhD

Licensed Psychotherapist

Founder, **Empty Arms Support Group**, Saddleback Church

Author, *In Heavenly Arms:*
Grieving the Loss and Healing the Wounds of Miscarriage

DEDICATION

To my loving husband, Rick, my devoted partner in life and our shared ministry,

To my precious children, Ryan and Avery, who brought and continue to bring immeasurable joy to my life, helping to heal after the heartbreaking loss of our first-born son, Matthew, and baby Hacker.

To my dear family no longer here on earth whose examples of living well have left indelible imprints on my heart.

To the families we have been blessed to meet through the Empty Arms ministry. It's been an honor to know you and your babies—their lives will never be forgotten.

And to my cherished friends and extended family, your love, support, comfort, and encouragement have truly been a blessing.

This book is dedicated to each of you for your unwavering support, love, and the light you've brought into my life. Your presence, both in the living and in the cherished memories of those who've passed, has been the inspiration behind this journey through grief, leading to the discovery of God's pathway to peace and ultimately finding

Hope in the Darkness.

CONTENTS

INTRODUCTION

I've written this book to help others find hope in times of personal darkness, keeping in mind that we all endure various seasons of life. Some seasons bring warmth, love, and happiness, while others bring challenges, introspection, and growth. This book addresses how to survive the colder seasons—those that present unbearable devastation from loss.

There are many kinds of loss, such as the loss of a loved one, a dream, a relationship, a job, a friend, or of health. This book is written out of a passion for helping others through any loss. It comes from the genuine and certain hope I have personally experienced throughout several devastating seasons of personal loss and darkness in my own life and the lives of my loved ones. I hope this book reflects God's love and hope: an effort to share how we can make it through the darkness with Him by our side—whether we realize He is there or not.

Karen

8:28

H

HOPE IN THE DARKNESS

INTRODUCTION

CHAPTER 1

HOW COME?

Why Me? Why Do Bad Things Happen?

How come? Why me? Why do bad things happen to good people? Understandably, we all ask questions along these lines when we endure difficult and dark times in life. But as common as these questions may be, there are some even deeper questions we should ask.

I have led grief and loss support groups alongside my husband, Rick, for nearly 30 years. As a result of much loss and heartbreak in my own life, I have asked these "How come?" and "Why me?" questions over and over again. What I have learned over the years is that there are healthier questions to ask, questions such as, "Why *not* me?" or "What am I supposed to *learn* or *do* in this situation?" and "How am I going to make it through this?"

In thinking about the difficult and unanswered questions in my life, I found Scripture to literally be a God-send for comfort, strength, forgiveness, and hope. Over the years, one verse has kept surfacing, tapping me on the shoulder, helping me to move forward:

> *And we know that in all things God works for the good of those who love him, who have been called according to his purpose.*
> *Romans 8:28 (NIV)*

However, I kept thinking, *How could the terrible and heartbreaking things I'm going through possibly be or lead to "good" as God promises?* I love God and believe I'm a good person, so why were so many bad things happening to me and the people I love? I needed answers to my questions and wanted the things I had been through to serve some purpose. I needed to find the "good" amid the "bad," which serves as the foundation of this book.

I will be sharing my story as well as the stories of others throughout this book. I will also reference Bible verses that have been helpful, hopeful, and meaningful to me. I like to use modern Bible translations rather than the standard King James version, which uses terms such as "thee" and "thou shalt not." All efforts have been made to acknowledge resources; however, some materials have been used over an extended period of time where origin is uncertain.

The numbers 8 2 8

As we embark on this journey together, I glance at my computer clock and see that it is 8:28 a.m. Coincidence? I don't think so! God never fails to show me how real He is and how He is always with me. In this book, I share examples of the many times throughout my life when God provided me with gifts and signs to show me that He is truly with me and that He is good. I can't even begin to count the many times God has led me to Romans 8:28.

For years, especially during some of my darkest days, I have been faced with the numbers 8 2 8. Nearly every day, I'll randomly glance at my bedside clock, phone, computer screen, or television, and those significant numbers will appear. I believe these are signs showing me that God was and is with me through everything, and He will use what I am going through for "good."

There are countless verses in the Bible that speak to me and bring me hope, especially Romans 8:28. It provides me with knowledge and the hope that God is good and that He will work out the details in my life for His purpose and plan. If you know God's character and truly seek Him, He promises that He is with us. He loves us and wants the best for us.

It is often hard to understand and see God's plan when we are going through difficult times. We wonder, *How can anything good possibly come from the situation?* To my surprise, God has continued to prove that He can and *will* work good in and through all the situations in my life, whether good or bad. This is not to say that all situations we face are good; it is simply to say that He can and does work good within all situations.

Loss in life is inevitable; we will all endure loss and darkness at some point. It is usually through our greatest trials—or, as I call it, our greatest darkness—that our greatest blessings come! As you endure dark times, you will witness first-hand how God reaches out to you even when you don't realize He is there. You can be assured by His great love for you and by His character that a future of hope and peace will emerge if you are open to finding solace and healing through Him. You will see His gifts in places and situations you never even imagined.

As you experience this book, I hope and pray that you will be able to work through some personal dark times and address some of your "How come" and "Why me?" questions. I hope you move toward a place of healing, acceptance, peace, hope, and purpose in and through the pain and difficult circumstances you encounter—and I am convinced you can, just as I and so many others have.

A Little About Me

I grew up in a middle-class home with two loving parents and an older sister and brother. I couldn't have asked for a healthier upbringing filled with love, respect, and faith. My parents were educators and school administrators, so there was always a high value placed on education and encouragement to do your best to succeed. Our home was filled with laughter, respect, honesty, creativity, responsibility, love, a lot of fun, and a strong foundation of family and faith.

Everything seemed to come pretty easy for me: I had a safe home, a loving family, and was blessed with many wonderful friends. I did well in school and enjoyed participating in plays, sports, cheerleading, and many other activities. Our family vacationed across the United States and Europe and went on annual water and snow skiing trips. We thoroughly enjoyed family, friends, and life together. I set off to college, where I was in a sorority and met some of my closest friends and a wonderful man named Rick.

At age twenty-five, Rick and I became husband and wife. We both landed good jobs and began building our life together. After two years of marriage, we decided it was time to start a family, and shortly after that decision, I became pregnant. I had a very easy pregnancy with minimal discomfort. We were so happy and excited at the thought of being parents. Everything seemed to go as planned until I went for a routine examination at my seven-month check-up. During the exam, we were told there might be something wrong with our baby and that additional tests were needed. I couldn't believe my ears and thought there must be a mistake. I felt my heart sink, and my head was spinning with questions. I quickly called Rick to tell him the news, and he rushed to meet me at the hospital for an in-depth ultrasound and a slew of tests.

After additional testing, we were completely unprepared for the news we received. We were told our precious baby had a severe heart condition—Hypoplastic Left Heart Syndrome—and probably wouldn't survive. Rick and I were completely shocked. The doctors wanted me to carry the baby to term (two very long months), hoping the other organs would develop enough to survive a possible heart surgery or transplant. We were devastated, and those next two months were almost unbearable as we faced the reality that our precious baby would most likely die.

Although Rick and I had been raised by parents who believed that faith and church were important, and who took us to church as children, we had not been regular church attendees as newlyweds. But as soon as we heard this devastating news, we decided to make a decision that changed our lives. We decided to run directly to God for strength, hope, comfort, and guidance. We prayed and trusted God to help us through this dark time we were experiencing.

The following two months were filled with doctor appointments and uncertainty. It was the holiday season; needless to say, it was tough to get into the spirit of Christmas with the fear of losing my precious baby looming over me. I was obviously very pregnant, so when I went out in public, people joyfully asked me questions like, "When is your baby due?" or "Is this your first?" These were all very innocent, well-meaning questions, but they were heartbreaking, knowing the condition of my baby. To avoid difficult situations in public, I ended up staying home and not venturing outside much for the remaining weeks. We kept very close to family and a few close friends whom we would invite to our home to help us get our minds off things. We watched movies, played games, talked, and enjoyed each other's company as much as we could, yet there was a constant heaviness hanging over us regardless of our efforts to redirect our thoughts.

Our son, Matthew Aaron Hacker, was born on January 20, 1990. The doctors had warned us that when babies with this type of heart condition are born, they typically look beautiful as if nothing were wrong. They were right: Matthew looked perfect. We thought, *How could this beautiful baby be taken away from us? He looks perfectly healthy!*

After the doctors ran many tests, they determined that Matthew could not be a candidate for heart surgery but that there may be a slim possibility of a heart transplant. In talking with the doctors further, we learned our baby would need a heart and lung transplant, which had rarely been done in infants at that time. I remember sitting at a long table in a meeting room with the medical team to discuss our options. I remember looking into the eyes of our primary doctor sitting across from me. I asked this man we had grown to respect and trust over the past few months, "If this was your baby, what would you do?" He paused for a moment, and his eyes welled up with tears. He answered, "I would let him go." As much as it pained us to even imagine losing Matthew, we realized we had to do the most unselfish thing for our baby. We had to let him go.

Matthew lived for a little over two days. We were with him continually, and when Matthew's heart stopped, I felt as if mine did, too. My heart was completely broken. I felt so empty and sad, and I didn't think I could ever be happy again. Leaving the hospital without my son and with empty arms was one of the most challenging things I would ever do.

I was unprepared for the immediate physical and emotional affects this devastating loss would have on me. I had just delivered a baby, so naturally, my body needed to heal after giving birth—a painful reminder that I gave birth with no joyful outcome. My breast milk came in, but I had no baby to feed. I was told I needed to bind myself to reduce the amount of milk flowing to my breasts, which was extremely uncomfortable and another painful reminder that my body had milk to give yet, no baby to feed. The baby's room was ready and waiting for the new arrival. It was a beautiful room filled with so many thoughtful gifts for our new baby. It was unbearable to see, so we just closed the door until we were ready to deal with it.

We decided to scatter Matthew's ashes on Mount Diablo, a mountaintop in Northern California, where we lived at the time. The day we chose, one week after Matthew was born, was a gray, stormy day. Rick and I climbed up to a sheltered spot on the mountain, where we held each other and cried. At one point, I looked up to the sky with outstretched arms and asked God to please give us a sign that we would be able to get through and overcome this nightmare. At that moment, the clouds parted, and a ray of sunshine beat down on us. With tears in our eyes, we both started chuckling in amazement and said, "Well, that's a pretty good sign!" We then scattered Matthew's ashes, prayed, and cried some more before heading down the mountain to my parent's house, where we were staying for a few days to recover and be cared for. As soon as we walked through the door, my mom told us there had been a perfect rainbow arching over the mountain the entire time we were on top.

Working through our grief during the following year was very difficult. I cried every day for six months and questioned how Rick could continue working and going about his day when I felt I could barely get out of bed each morning. After several months, we decided to get some grief counseling, at which point we began to slowly heal, and a glimmer of hope for the future started to appear. When we became stronger, we thought it would be healing if we could somehow help others through similar situations, but at the time, we weren't sure how we might be able to do that. We wanted Matthew's short life and everything we had been through to serve some purpose and provide something good for us and for others. We didn't want Matthew's life, albeit only two days, to be meaningless.

I found out I was pregnant again on what would have been Matthew's first birthday. Rick and I felt God gave us such a special blessing on a day we dreaded. Instead of a day of sadness in remembering and reliving the pain of losing Matthew, God gave us a beautiful gift of hope for a new baby. We were both very excited about the news but also terrified. Unfortunately, our fears became a reality when six weeks later, I miscarried, and once again, our hopes and dreams for a family were shattered.

I truly felt I would never be happy again until I could hold in my arms and bring home one of my babies. Everywhere I looked, I would see babies and pregnant women. It seemed everyone around me was able to have a baby except me. I felt inadequate, embarrassed, envious, jealous, sad, fearful, depressed, and helpless. Many of these emotions were foreign to me, and I wasn't sure what to do with them, but I kept moving forward one day at a time, trying to surround myself with friends, family, faith, and prayer. It wasn't until years later that I learned that all those emotions were a normal part of grief.

My wish for another baby finally became a reality in 1992, when our son, Ryan, was born, and then two years later, his sister, Avery, was born. Both are perfectly healthy and incredible blessings in our lives.

Despite our joy in our two children, we kept questioning why we had gone through such pain and grief, and in 1995, we were given some answers.

We had just moved to Mission Viejo in Southern California, and our dearest friends invited us to attend their very large church, Saddleback Valley Community Church. We went and were amazed. That morning, the message was how God has a plan for our lives and how we must be patient, waiting for things to happen in His time, not necessarily our time. Several couples gave testimonies about how they had lost children to miscarriage, stillbirth, and infant death and how they had found healing through a support group called Empty Arms which had been started by Shari Bridgman, a marriage and family therapist and member of Saddleback Church. They shared how they had worked through their grief and gained a feeling of hope for the future, trusting God's plan for their lives.

Rick and I were extremely emotional throughout the service. Afterward, we spoke with some couples who shared their stories. I just knew we had to be a part of this church and this group. We immediately joined the church, went through the 8-week Empty Arms sessions as participants, and trained to become Empty Arms facilitators. And in 1997, we were asked to head up the Empty Arms Ministry. Since then, Rick and I have been leading and counseling parents and family members who have suffered through the loss of babies due to miscarriage, stillbirth, or infant death. We have also trained others to start loss support groups in their churches and communities.

There is much more to my story of grief and loss, which includes the loss of seven immediate family members in a very short time, which I will share in the coming chapters. With so much loss, I kept questioning God, asking, "Why do I need to experience so much loss?" and "What am I supposed to do with it?"

I had been teaching about loss and grief for many years and felt as though I understood grief better than most. I knew it all too well—far more than I ever wanted to. But just because I understood it didn't mean I didn't have to go through it. Grief hurts, and loss is painful. No one can simply get *over* grief. You have to go *through* it. So, I have become a grief expert of sorts, without ever wanting to become one. I had never considered writing a book, but God has made it abundantly clear that I needed to write this book, so I am here, writing out of pure obedience to God, and for the empathy and love I have for others who are hurting in the same ways I was.

I also wrote this book while drawing inspiration from the very questions mentioned earlier. One day, while driving to my weekly women's Bible study group, I was praying and asking God what I was supposed to do with everything I had endured. With so much loss, I thought there just had to be a reason for it to make any sense. At that very moment, a song came on the radio. It was a song I had never heard before, and I can't say I have heard it on the radio since, but it brought me to tears. The basic message was "my" verse:

And we know that in all things God works for the good of those who love him, who have been called according to his purpose.
Romans 8:28 (NIV)

It was the same verse message and verse numbers that had been showing up to me over and over again for many years. At that very moment, God gave me a vision of a book that I later turned into the exact cover of this book, *8:28 Hope in the Darkness*. I started laughing and crying and said out loud to God, "Really? You want me to write a book?" I don't have a doctorate or master's degree in psychology, psychiatry, theology, or counseling, nor do I have any other degrees or letters behind my name. I'm just a person who has been through much loss and has tried to help others understand and work through grief for many years. I have never considered writing a book or considered myself to be much of a writer, for that matter. I must therefore give all credit to God because I know that it is only with Him by my side that I have completed this book, or as I call it, "His" book. So, as I wrote this, I trusted another one of His promises:

For I can do everything through Christ, who gives me strength.
Philippians 4:13 (NLT)

By sharing my experiences with those of you who want to help others through loss or those traveling through the darkness of loss yourselves, I hope you will find peace and hope to help work through, understand, and manage grief and loss.

The following chapters explore the "how" and "why" questions. You will have the opportunity to address those painful questions and work toward transforming your pain into peace and purpose. You will read stories of loss and how others chose to use their pain to help others gain an understanding of how God and faith play such an important role throughout our lives. Dare to join in this journey of finding peace in your dark times and hope for the future by participating in the coming chapters.

Before moving on to Chapter 2, reflect on and explore your answers to the following questions:

✧ How am I going to get through this in a healthy way?

✧ What am I going to do with these experiences?

✧ How can this situation help me grow or help others in similar situations?

✧ What is God's plan, and how do I turn this situation into something good?

✧ Will I ever be happy again?

✧ Do I trust God?

Think about these things and take some time to write down your thoughts, which we will turn to in later chapters.

8:28

O

H**O**PE IN THE DARKNESS

CHAPTER 2
OPEN UP

Open Up - Revealing Leads to Healing

I've listened to Pastor Rick Warren[1] of Saddleback Church repeat the words, "The first step to healing is revealing your feelings," time and time again, and each time, their deep-seated truth becomes more apparent to me. (Pastor Rick is not only a trusted spiritual advisor for many people worldwide, but he has also experienced significant loss.) As we work through this journey, we must open up and be honest with ourselves and others about our feelings. This is especially true if you want to heal or help others heal and work through difficult times.

That being said, opening up and allowing ourselves to be vulnerable isn't easy; it takes courage to face head-on what we are going through. But to process our emotions and make sense of them, we need to first identify and feel them. Too many times, people try to stuff, hide or ignore their feelings. Unfortunately, if emotions are not dealt with, they may come out in other ways and are later linked to unresolved grief, such as anger, illness, bitterness, anxiety, and depression. Through our years of grief counseling, we have seen situations where people become stuck in an emotion and find it difficult to move forward. Feelings must be addressed and dealt with before moving toward healing and finding peace and purpose in what you have experienced.

One of the first exercises we begin with during our group sessions is writing or telling your story from beginning to end. We ask participants to share details about their situation—their hopes, shattered dreams, guilt, anxiety, jealousy, fears, or whatever is weighing them down or preying on their minds. Hopefully, you have someone who will listen and not judge or try to fix the situation when you share your story.

Whether you are spiritual or not, God is always available to listen if you can't think of a "safe" person to share with. In going through the tough times in my life, besides sharing with my husband, close family members, or friends, I try to continually seek God for comfort, guidance, and answers to my many questions.

It is not uncommon for people to question God's motives when bad things happen. Many blame God or feel He is punishing them for previous choices, but that is not the God I know or choose to believe in. The God I know is all about love, comfort, forgiveness, peace, and hope.

We often seek answers beyond ourselves and look to God or a "higher power." We need to understand why or how this could have happened, so we search for answers. We tend to blame someone or something for the bad things that happen in our lives. Some blame God, some blame others, and some blame themselves for what happened. We have an innate desire to seek answers to our questions in hopes that these answers will allow us to wrap things up and put our grief and loss away.

Unfortunately, we are not always given answers to our questions here on earth. We live in a world of good and evil, and we don't always know why God allows certain things to happen in our lives and the lives of others. We can't always control what happens to us, but we *can* choose how we react to our circumstances. Sometimes, while going through those tough times, it is hard not to have a "pity party," *but* over time (and if we are open), we can reflect on those difficult times and see how God was with us and how He carried us through those most difficult times. If we are open to it, we can trust that He has a plan, and that peace and hope will prevail in our future through it all.

We all have different perceptions of who God is. The God I know is a loving God whom I can go to with anything. I can share my hopes, thoughts, fears, desires, frustrations, and needs with Him. I can share whatever is on my heart at any given moment. If you have never talked to God, I would suggest talking to him like you would talk to a friend. You don't need to use antiquated or flowery words like "thou shalt not," "thee," or "thine." If you don't believe in God, try asking for help with your unbelief and ask God to reveal Himself to you in ways that make sense. Whether it be through a friend, lyrics in a song, a beautiful gift of nature, something you read in a book, or something a stranger says, I truly believe that if your heart is open and you start looking and asking Him to reveal himself to you, He will. If you seek and ask Him into your life, He will show up in ways you would never have imagined.

God is bigger than our grief, sorrow, pain, and any problem we will ever face. Life is hard, and if we truly live life well and fully, we will have wonderful times, but we will also have difficult times. We will experience so many emotions in a lifetime—from ultimate joy to the heaviest sorrow. The Bible shares how the Lord is close to the brokenhearted, and He saves the crushed in spirit, and that the Lord will deliver us from evil. The Bible also tells us we will have glory and suffering in this life, but in our suffering, endurance, character, and hope are strengthened, and in all things, God will work good.

Grief and sorrow are natural emotions when experiencing loss, so it is perfectly acceptable to feel those emotions and the many other emotions associated with loss, as long as you identify and share your feelings, as this leads to healthy healing. Don't try to mask or hide your emotions. Emotions are healthy; you must experience the emotions of grief to get to the place of acceptance and hope for the future. Research has shown that the cause of many psychological issues today may result from avoidance of dealing with negative emotions.[2] This can be surprising because attempting to avoid negative emotions may seem reasonable. Negative emotions aren't usually pleasant. We live in a world of instant gratification with a goal to "feel good," so we think to ourselves, *I don't want to feel bad, so I am going to do everything possible to stay busy and bury my feelings, so I don't feel them.* Avoiding negative emotions can buy short-term gain, but long-term pain is the price.

An example may be a person who, under stress, decides to have a drink to relieve the stress or pain they are experiencing. In the short term, it may work, but the next day when bad feelings come again, they drink again. If this becomes a daily occurrence, another more significant problem may arise; you may develop an addiction that stems from unresolved avoidance of emotions. People with Post-Traumatic

Stress Disorder (PTSD) often try to avoid or "stuff" their feelings. It has been found that refusing to acknowledge or address pain can exacerbate symptoms of PTSD.[3] Avoidance may provide relief in the beginning stages of grief, but it can turn into a much greater problem down the road.

Everyone will grieve in this lifetime. We and everyone we know are terminal, so it is inevitable that when we lose those we love, we will grieve. If our marriage falls apart, we will grieve. If we get a diagnosis from the doctor that we have cancer, we will grieve. It may not be grief due to the loss of life, but it may be grief due to the loss of a dream of how things used to be or the loss of the family unit you had once dreamed of. It isn't a matter of *if* we will grieve; it is a matter of *when* and *how* we will grieve.

What I have learned over 30 years of grief counseling is that the ones who deal with grief head-on are the ones who get through grief and arrive at the other side in a healthier state. Those who try to hide, ignore, and "go around" their grief instead of going through it tend to have more difficulties as time goes on. As mentioned, grief can come in many forms if not dealt with initially. Resentment, bitterness, blame, anger, stress, and illness (both emotional and physical) are quite common effects of grief, and a person can get stuck in some of those effects by not addressing their pain from the start. No one wants to get stuck in that negative cycle, so we must do what we can to avoid getting trapped.

The exercise below will help you begin revealing and sharing your story to enable you to start your journey of healing and hope.

EXERCISE 1: Write your story in detail and share it with a safe person willing to listen. Provide dates, times, and the people who were involved. Describe everything from beginning to end. Include every detail you can think of—the sights, smells, memories, and lost hopes and dreams. What are the frustrations or feelings of guilt, anger, sadness, or pain that you experienced? Get your thoughts out of your head by putting them on paper, and don't forget to have some tissues handy because, more than likely, there may be tears. Grief and loss involve a multitude of emotions that may seem like a jumbled mess swirling around in your head. Review **REFERENCE A** below. How many of these emotions and feelings of grief can you relate to? Use this visual to identify and help get some thoughts and emotions out of your head and down on paper.

This exercise may provide some surprises. Once we start writing things down, other thoughts and feelings may emerge, which is a good start. Only through identifying our feelings can true healing begin.

REFERENCE A

Web of Emotions and Feelings of Grief

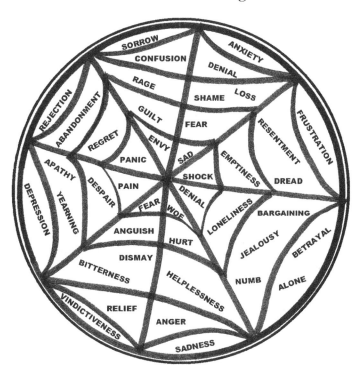

If you are like most people, you will find that many of the emotions shown will fit with what you are going through, or, if not, you may experience them later. The key is understanding that the emotions shown in the "web of emotions" are natural emotions associated with grief. It is helpful to see the feelings you may be experiencing and realize those emotions aren't signs that you are losing your mind. There is no need to feel guilt or shame in feeling some of these emotions. These are all very normal emotions of grief, and it is okay to experience them.

So many times, I felt like I was going to lose my mind, as if I were stuck in a tornado of grief and overwhelming emotions—all coming at me simultaneously from every angle. During my first real experience with grief and loss after losing Matthew, I experienced emotions I had never felt before; sometimes, they were emotions I was embarrassed to feel. Feeling envious when seeing other moms with babies. Feeling depressed and jealous when I found out a friend was pregnant instead of being happy for them. Feeling like a failure each month I didn't become pregnant. Each month became another, more intense loss the longer it took me to get pregnant again. Envy, failure, jealousy, and depression were emotions I had not experienced before, so I wasn't quite sure what to do with them. Those foreign emotions, combined with feelings most people consider "typical" when going through a loss (such as sadness, pain, sorrow, and missing someone), made me feel like I was losing my mind. But I wasn't. I was just grieving. The emotions of grief and loss are some of the darkest times we will ever go through. Grief is normal and expected. You can't go around it, over, or under it. You have to go through it. But it was at this point in my journey, as the multitude of emotions swirling through my head felt almost unbearable, that I knew I needed to get help.

I cannot express how helpful writing things down on paper or your computer can be. It can feel as if a huge weight is lifted once you get some thoughts and emotions organized and out of your head. We saw physical evidence of this through one of our Empty Arms sessions. At the fifth weekly meeting (out of eight), one of the grieving moms came into the meeting room looking like a completely different person.

In previous sessions, she had looked pale, sad, worn out, and broken, but at this meeting, she had a lightness that we had not seen before. Everyone in the session noticed the difference in her. When we asked what had happened and why she looked so different, she told us that she had taken our challenge to write down her thoughts, feelings, and emotions. She went out of town to take some time by herself and ended up writing for three days straight. She said she went through at least ten boxes of tissue, and writing out her emotions was the best thing she had done for herself in a long time. She felt relief, healing, and hope for the future for the first time in months.

Surely, this type of exercise won't always have this result. Still, this example shows what a huge benefit it was to this woman, and we have repeatedly witnessed how writing our emotions can be hugely beneficial for our well-being. Once you can identify and understand that your feelings are a normal part of grief, you can address them, feel them, and work through them.

Grief is entirely individual for everyone. You may feel many intense emotions all at the same time, yet someone with a similar loss may not. We like to use the visual of **REFERENCE A, "Web of Emotions," as shown on page 27**, rather than a step-by-step process to work through grief because we have learned that grief is messy. The emotions and process of grief are different for everyone. Grief is hard; it is individual and it takes time.

After a devastating or tragic loss, and if one is healthily working through their grief, it typically takes one to two years to feel a sense of peace or see a glimmer of hope for future happiness. People often long to be "normal" again after a loss, but what they may not understand is that from the moment something devastating happens, their lives will be forever changed. They will never again have what they once knew, but they will instead have a "new normal," which we will discuss in Chapter 14. For me and many others, over time, I have seen many blessings in my circumstances and have come to a place of peace in realizing why certain things had to happen as they did, and I can now honestly say I'm happy in my new normal. It's not that I don't still experience times of sadness over the things and people I have lost, but I have come to a place of peace and acceptance where I can also experience hope and happiness.

Many people have heard of the five stages of grief developed by Elisabeth Kübler-Ross in her book, *On Death and Dying*[4]. She originally developed five stages to describe the process patients with a terminal illness go through when they learn that they (or a loved one) are dying. Denial, Anger, Bargaining, Depression, and Acceptance, known as **DABDA,** are the main stages Kubler-Ross outlines; however, many additional feelings and emotions may be associated with each stage.

Denial

The first reaction is denial. In this stage, a person often believes the diagnosis is somehow a mistake and clings to a false, preferable reality: This can't be happening to me. This emotion typically occurs at the beginning of loss—when you first get the word that you have cancer, or when your boss tells you to pack up your things, or when the police officer comes to your door informing you about the accident, or when you learn that your spouse has been unfaithful. Many people go into a "denial" phase and can't or don't want to believe what is happening to them.

Anger

Once through denial, the person accepts the loss, and they often become angry. Responses of someone during this phase sound something like this: "Why me?" or "It's not fair!" They may also want to place blame and have someone to be angry at, asking, "Who is responsible for this?" or "What kind of God would allow this to happen?" Anger often occurs when you can't make sense of your loss. We have found three typical objects of people's anger: God, themselves, or others. During one of our sessions, we had a very angry group and realized we needed to add a session devoted strictly to Anger, which I will discuss more in Chapter 5, entitled, "I'm Angry!"

Bargaining

The third stage involves hoping someone can avoid or change the cause of their grief. Usually, there is some negotiation for extended life, for example, in exchange for a changed lifestyle. People facing less severe trauma can bargain or seek compromise. Examples may include a terminally ill person who "negotiates with God" to keep them around long enough to attend their daughter's wedding. There may be an attempt to bargain for more time, to live longer in exchange for a reformed lifestyle, or to beg for a trade, such as "Let me die instead!" or "Please don't let my wife have cancer; I will do anything you want me to do! I will change and become a better person, but please don't let her have cancer!" Bargaining is typically directed toward God in hopes of saving a marriage, a job, or even one's life.

Depression

In the fourth stage, people often despair at recognizing their mortality. The individual may become silent, refuse visitors, and spend much of their time mournfully and often sullenly. Attitudes such as the following can occur: *I don't care about anything. I just want to be left alone* or *I'm so sad; why bother with anything?* These thoughts can turn tragic, such as *I'm going to die soon, so what's the point?* or *I miss my loved one; why go on?*

It is easy to spiral into feeling sorry for yourself—a "pity party"—and sometimes even to get stuck in depression when you can't see hope for the future. Depression can imprison you in your grief and cause you to be unloving toward other family members and friends, leading to further losses and even self-harm.

When you continually have negative thoughts about yourself and others, it may be time to seek professional help or join a support group. As challenging as it may be to make that first phone call, if you are considering whether you need help, then you probably do! Once you make that call, you will most likely be assured of two things. First, you are experiencing the normal emotions of grief and loss; second, making the call was the right thing for you to do.

Acceptance

In this stage, people begin to accept their situation: *It's going to be okay. I still feel the pain and sadness over my loss, but I will accept the reality of it.* At this point, a person gains a healthy acceptance of the situation and is ready to move forward. You don't forget the pain experienced, but you can use that pain to make you stronger. You may even come to a place where you can use your circumstances for a higher purpose, such as helping others in similar situations. At this stage, you begin having a sense of peace and experience some joyful times in life again.

In the book, *Finding Meaning, The Sixth Stage of Grief* by David Kessler, the Kübler-Ross model was expanded to include any form of personal loss: losses such as the death of a loved one, loss of a job or income, a significant rejection, divorce or end of a relationship, drug addiction, incarceration, injury, disease, or an infertility diagnosis. Even minor losses were included, such as a loss of insurance coverage. Kessler has also proposed "Meaning" as a sixth stage of grief, which goes along with finding a purpose as a result of a loss. This is where we can look at the situation from a different perspective and see some positive outcomes.

In 2020, during an interview with the *Harvard Business Review*[6], Kessler applied the five stages of grief to our responses to Covid-19, stating, "Understanding the stages of grief is a start. But whenever I talk about this, I have to remind people that the stages aren't linear and may not happen in this order. It's not a map, but it provides some scaffolding for this unknown world. There's **denial**, which we saw a lot of early on: This virus won't affect us. There's **anger**: You're making me stay home and taking away my activities. There's **bargaining**: Okay, if I social distance everything will be better, right? There's **sadness**: I don't know when this will end. And finally, there's acceptance. This is happening; I have to figure out how to proceed. **Acceptance**, as you might imagine, is where the power lies. We find control in acceptance. I can wash my hands. I can keep a safe distance. I can learn how to work virtually."

Meaning as the sixth stage wasn't addressed in the example above, but if we think about it, we can see there are positive things that came as a result of the Covid-19 pandemic. Companies and employees learned that productivity could be achieved as easily at home as it can in an office. Businesses, families, and friends learned how to communicate and find new ways to be together via Zoom and Google Meets. Families learned how to work and teach their children from home in new and different ways. The neighborhood ladies I've seen walking alone for years were walking with their husbands. Fathers were playing basketball with their kids in their driveways. The skies were bluer, with fewer cars on the road, leading to fewer car accidents.

That being said, I acknowledge that Covid-19 also caused incredible grief in many ways and may be why you picked up this book in the first place. I am so sorry to those who experienced loss during this time. Covid-19 has been devastating. As with all grief, however, we should strive to reach a point where we can look for the good.

Kessler has confirmed what we have observed and noted previously: grief is a highly individualized experience. People who are grieving do not necessarily go through the stages in the same order or even experience them all. Many additional emotions and feelings are attributed to grief and loss, as shown in the **"Web of Emotions" (REFERENCE A),** which can be experienced multiple times throughout the healing process. Since the experience of grief is so variable and individual, it is dangerous to compare yourself to others in the grieving process.

EXERCISE 2: Now, look at **REFERENCE A** again on Page 27. Select five or six emotions that stick out to you and write them on paper. Write a sentence for each word on a separate paper and describe how this emotion is personal to you.

Here are a few examples to guide you in this exercise:

Example Emotion: Envy

Personal to me: I feel **envy** every time I see large families together. I miss my family so much, and I long to have large family gatherings like we used to. The holidays and special occasions feel so small and lonely now.

Example Emotion: Frustration

Personal to me: I feel **frustrated** because I have no control over the situation, and I like to be in control. I'm **frustrated** that no one understands what I'm going through.

After you identify some of your feelings on paper, spend time expressing them. You can express them in various ways, depending on your gifts and personality.

Here are some ideas:

⬦ Continue writing about your emotions by journaling how you feel each day.

⬦ Continue to share how you are feeling with a safe person or persons.

⬦ Express your feelings through art and creativity. Paint, make music, draw, compose, sculpt, or write poetry.

✧ Pray! Ask God to help you work through specific emotions you are experiencing. For non-believers, ask the Lord to help you with your unbelief and to show himself to you: "If you are there, Lord, please help comfort, guide, and get me through this."

> *The Lord is near the brokenhearted and saves the crushed spirit.*
> *Psalm 34:18 (NIV)*

Though we are using writing exercises in this book, you likely have talents unique to your personality that may be better expressed in other ways. Take time to express your emotions in the best way for you! Now is the time to be selfish and be good to yourself, so that you can heal and move to a place of acceptance. Give yourself permission for self-care.

Learning and growing through loss

As difficult as it is to go through tragedy and loss, the experiences of loss help form the person we become. Often, it is through the most challenging times that we learn and grow the most. If everything were always easy and perfect for us, we really wouldn't learn much about living life. Our true character is revealed through hardships and turmoil, and life's lessons are learned.

At times, I have told God that I didn't want or need any more "character-building" trials or learning lessons. However, I know that in those trials, He is with me and that through those trials, I am being transformed into the person God wants me to be. This gives me hope. If we want something we don't yet have, we must prayerfully, patiently, and confidently wait for it. With that knowledge, I pray my experiences can bring help and hope to others.

It is hard to explain how I know God is with me, but I just do. He provides me with constant gifts to show me that He is there. It is a feeling of certainty that, at times, is unexplainable, and that is the essence of faith.

> *Now faith is the assurance of things hoped for,*
> *the conviction of things not seen.*
> *Hebrews 11:1 (ESV)*

Even though I can't see God, I know He is there because I observe Him working all around me, whether through people, nature, answered prayers, music, or unexpected peace.

The following is another verse we have used in our support groups and one I have clung to during challenging times.

We also rejoice in our sufferings, because we know that suffering produces perseverance; perseverance, character, and character, hope.
Romans 5:3–5 (NIV)

There is hope in these words because we are assured that He is with us and carrying us through our times of darkness. It is through those times that we grow stronger. He is with us always, cares about and loves us, and gives us peace and hope for the future.

I know this to be true because I have lived it, and others can also testify to it. I never in my wildest dreams would have thought I would be able to endure the things I have endured, but each time a difficult situation comes up, I am given the strength to get through it, and each time, I become stronger. I gain more empathy, compassion, love, and hope for the future.

I know I have grown through my trials; my character, strength, compassion, empathy, and patience have all developed because of the experiences I have been through. I would not be who I am today had it not been for what I have gone through. Looking back at my life, I can see how and why certain things had to happen as they did. I know that there is a plan in all of it. In looking at the circumstances and choices I made over the years, I know that some of my choices weren't necessarily "good" and may have had some immediate consequences that weren't pleasant at the time. Yet, I can look back and see how God has turned my choices and circumstances into something good. Whether it was a breakup, a decision about which college to attend, a cut from a team, the loss of a job, a car accident, the loss of family members, or anything that felt difficult or like a loss at the time, I can see how positive things came out of each of those situations. If you honestly examine your life, particularly exploring the difficult times you have already been through, I'm confident that you will see how blessings and good things have come from them. There is always something to be thankful for, although it's sometimes hard to see during it.

Now that you have begun to examine some of the emotions you may be feeling and shared your story with someone safe, the next chapter considers friends and family who try to be helpful but sometimes fall short of our needs and expectations.

8:28

P

HOPE IN THE DARKNESS

CHAPTER 3

PEOPLE CAN HELP OR HINDER

Family and Friends

People are generally good and want to help, but they often don't know what to do or say in situations of loss and tragedy. We need to allow each other to grieve in our own personal way, and sometimes, we need to educate others about what our needs may be. This can be confusing because sometimes, we don't know what we need or what would make us feel better.

With so many emotions and feelings swirling around in our heads as a result of grief and loss, other people may find it genuinely hard to know what would be most helpful. Some days, for example, we may want to talk about the situation, and other days we may not want to engage in any mention of it. There may be times when we want to be held and comforted, and other times when we just want to be left alone. Since people usually don't know what to say or how to react, they may need some training.

People who want to help can fall short and may even unintentionally end up hurting more than helping. I'll never forget when an acquaintance approached me when we found out I was pregnant for the second time after losing Matthew and said, "Maybe this time you will take better care of yourself." Although I know I was not responsible for Matthew's heart condition, this was devastating to hear. To think that someone thought I might have been responsible and stir up those doubts in my head was heartbreaking, to say the least. Did he not understand my pain? My unreasonable guilt? No, he didn't. I'm sure he meant well and maybe even regretted his comment, which may have been blurted out in a moment of nervousness and not knowing what to say. Similarly, when we announced our third pregnancy after losing our second baby to miscarriage, the same gentleman came up to us, slapped Rick on the back, and boldly stated, "Third time's a charm!"

One of the most painful comments made to me was when a family member, who chose abortion over keeping her baby, tried to console me by sharing that she knew how I felt because she, too, had lost a baby. I know she was trying to help, but she had a choice to keep her baby, and I didn't. I knew she was hurting over her choice many years prior, but she had no idea what I was feeling. Since I hadn't walked in her shoes, I wouldn't presume to know the pain she had been carrying for many years, but the comparison to my pain seemed so contradictory.

Some quickly say, "Oh, I know how you feel," and often add the word "exactly." So many times, I wanted to say, "Uh, no. You have no idea how I feel!" It was refreshing when someone said, "I can't imagine what you are feeling, but I'm here for you if you need to talk," or "How can I best help support you during this?" or simply, "I'm so sorry."

People so desperately want to help but don't know how to offer practical support when friends or family are in pain and dealing with difficult situations. With the losses we have been through, we have had so many wonderful family members, friends, and neighbors provide practical help with meals, cleaning our house, mowing our lawn, planting flowers in our yard, and doing laundry. They took care of our home and pets when we were out of town, provided help with memorial services, and drove our kids to and from school.

One of the nurses who helped us so much gave me a gift certificate for a massage and spa day at a beautiful resort nearby. Unfortunately, many people aren't as fortunate when it comes to the help and comfort they may need and desire. Moreover, many of us may find it hard to accept such generosity, but we need to be better at accepting help when things are offered. Offering practical ways to help and comfort are expressions of love and should be accepted as a gift. In receiving the gifts of care, we are not only helping ourselves, but we are also helping those who offer help. It gives them a place and purpose in the situation, too. Another act of comfort for someone who is grieving is just to be present, so they know they are cared for and loved. Sometimes, it isn't a matter of saying the right words, but being present with someone in pain.

As the saying goes, "When the going gets tough, the tough get going." However, I like to use a different spin on this saying, and have found it more meaningful: "When the going gets tough, the tough come in." The people who come in and are willing to tough it out with you truly make the difference. So often, people don't know what to say, so they say nothing at all. It is the proverbial elephant in the room. Everyone knows it is there, but no one wants to mention it for fear of upsetting others or drawing attention to what everyone is thinking about. People somehow believe you won't think about whatever you are going through if they don't bring it up. What they don't realize is that, most likely, you are thinking about the subject every day and all day long.

One reason our most difficult situations in life can be so challenging and painful is that the people we expect to understand and comfort us end up disappointing and hurting us simply by how they handle the situation. Sometimes, people say hurtful words in their attempt to help, or they say nothing at all and make you feel worse simply by how they look at you. They gaze at you in pity with eyes begging you to be better and back to "normal." And other times, people are overly bold and tell you how you should behave and that you need to "get over it" because they see long-term grief as something negative and potentially harmful.

One such instance of an insensitive attempt to help and push to get over it was from a coworker when Rick worked for a large toy company. Each year, there was a trade show called Toy Fair in New York where the most prominent vendors and retailers would come to show and buy their new products for the year. Toy Fair happened to fall just three weeks after we lost Matthew, but Rick had to attend since it was the major buying event of the year. The show consisted of very high-power sales expectations in a rah-rah-type atmosphere. There was no place for sadness: Everyone had to be upbeat and "on."

For some reason, Rick's boss thought it would be a good idea for Rick to "get back in the saddle" and be the "pit boss" for one of the days. The pit boss was the one who organized and set the tone for the day. Rick needed to have high power, elevated energy, and get everyone pumped up for the day. Of course, that was the last thing Rick's mind or body was prepared for; in his boss' mind, three weeks had been long enough for Rick to fully grieve and return to work. Crazy, huh?

When Rick questioned the role he had been placed in for the day, his boss told him that what Rick had been through wasn't a tragedy and that he needed to "get over it." Rick's boss had a friend who had passed away a few days prior and had left behind a wife with two young children. He told Rick that his friend's situation was a tragedy. He said that Rick should feel lucky that Matthew only lived a few short days and that it would have been so much worse if he had lived longer and then died. I know Rick's boss was grieving over the loss of his friend and didn't understand the lack of compassion and empathy he was heaping on Rick, but those comments were extremely painful to us both.

One of the most important gifts we can give when someone is grieving is simply acknowledging and validating the pain and emotions they may be feeling. There are no magic words to say. No one can "fix" the situation, so simply acknowledging the pain and permitting feelings of sadness, hurt, or frustration can be very helpful to someone who is grieving. It is healing to be heard and acknowledged, so acknowledgment is one of the greatest gifts we can give someone struggling with pain and grief.

The following are some ideas of how to support someone grieving regarding what to say (or what not to say).

What to Say

1. "I'm sorry."
2. "I'm here for you if you want to talk. I have plenty of time to listen."

3. "This must be so painful."

4. "I'm so sad for your loss."

5. "You are in my thoughts and prayers."

6. "This must be terribly hard for you and your family."

7. "I'm so sorry you are going through this"

8. "You can call me anytime. I'm here for you no matter how early or late."

   (Only use this statement if there can be sincere follow-through)

9. "I love you, and I'm here for you. Please let me know what I can do to help."

10. "I'm here, and I want to listen."

11. "Tell me about _____ (insert loved one's name here)."

12. Say nothing at all. Just offering your presence with a hug or touch of understanding can be all that is needed.

13. Simply say you have no words to express your sadness, given the situation.

What Not to Say

1. "It's all happened for the best."

2. "Don't worry; you will feel better soon."

3. "Now you have an angel in heaven watching over you."

4. "Everyone goes through loss; you will be fine."

5. "They are in a better place."

6. "It was God's will."

7. "You're young. You still time to find another husband/wife or have other children."

8. "It could be worse—like what happened to _____" (Rule of thumb: don't compare situations).

9. "God needed _____ (your loved one's name) with Him in heaven."

10. "This was God's way of saying something was wrong."

11. "At least you are alive."

12. "You must forget this ever happened and get on with your life."

13. "They would have wanted it this way." (And conversely, "They wouldn't want you to be sad.")

14. "It's time to get over it and move on."

15. "I understand." (Only if you have not had a similar experience.)

Another hint: Never start a sentence with the words "at least." Whenever a sentence begins with "at least," I know it isn't going to be good: "At least it happened now, before…", "At least you are young and…", "At least you have your health," "At least you have another child to love and care for," "At least…" Ugh!

Other Practical Ways to Help

1. Be supportive—visit or call to say, "I love and care about you and want to help. What would be most helpful for you today?"

2. With the loss of a child, treat the bereaved couple equally. Men need as much support as women.

3. Be available. Providing a meal, doing errands, cleaning the house, mowing the lawn, or babysitting are all things that need to be done, but all these things can seem overwhelming for someone who is grieving.

4. When a baby or child is lost, allow the parents to talk about them. Ask but don't pry. Just as parents love to talk about their living children, so do parents whose children are no longer here. They may want to share special memories or lost hopes and dreams. It is important to hear others speak their child's name.

5. Learn about the grieving process. The first book I read after losing my son was a book that was given to me called *When Bad Things Happen to Good People*[7] by Harold S. Kushner. It helped me realize that I wasn't alone in the feelings I was feeling. It helped me understand that God wasn't punishing me for any reason and that having doubts and fears after loss is normal. Other helpful books include *A Grief Observed*[8] by CS Lewis and *Don't Sing Songs to a Heavy Heart – How to relate to those who are suffering*[9] by Kenneth Haugk, Ph.D. A book that three friends recently read and recommended after losing their sons to suicide and health issues is *A Grace Disguised – How the Soul Grows Through Loss*[10] by Jerry Sittser. Many excellent books

are written to help understand the emotions of grief, each with a unique perspective from the individual(s) who created them. For additional resources listing additional titles that may interest you, please check www.828HOPE.com.

6. Don't be afraid to talk about or let others know you are thinking about their loss. Parents never forget the loss of a child. Brothers and sisters never forget the loss of a sibling, and we never forget the loss of our parents. Someone who has lost a loved one doesn't forget important dates or special memories. Letting them know you remember is comforting, especially on significant dates such as birthdays, holidays, due dates, and anniversaries. (Note: there are special months and dates specific to losing a loved one. It is extremely comforting to know someone is lighting a candle for or thinking of them on those emotional days.)

7. Be liberal with touching someone who is grieving, assuming they've given consent that it is okay to do so. People often need contact showing love and care. A hug, a touch on the shoulder, or a squeeze of the hand can be very comforting.

8. Send a card or note letting them know you are thinking about them every few weeks throughout the following year.

9. Help them address a surviving child's loss and grief by sending them picture books to read together. A few that come highly recommended are *The Invisible String*[11] by Patrice Karst, *My Yellow Balloon*[12] by Tiffany Papageorge, and *The Rhino Who Swallowed a Storm*[13] by LeVar Burton.

If you are struggling with grief and loss, another helpful way to let the people around you understand your needs is to write a letter explaining exactly what you hope for and expect from friends and family. Remember, your friends and family want to help but often feel helpless because they don't know what will be most helpful to you.

Exercise 3 can help you identify and share your needs and provide concrete ways your loved ones can help.

EXERCISE 3: Write a letter to family and friends, in which, for example, you:

- Describe what you have experienced and how you feel about it.

- Let people know what they can expect from you in your current state.

- Give friends permission to discuss it or instruct them on what they can do to help.

- Let them know what is needed and when. Share some of the dos and don'ts from the above lists (see "What to Say" and "What Not to Say").

- Share your current struggles with your grief and how you may have difficulties with the following:

  a. Understanding the many emotions that grief brings and, as a result, feeling emotionally unbalanced.

  b. Coping with feelings of guilt, anger, and jealousy.

  c. Dealing with normal daily functions due to lack of energy or desire.

  d. Deciding what to do with our loved one's belongings.

  e. Understanding our grief individually, as a couple, and/or as a family unit.

  f. Participating in family celebrations.

  g. Seeing babies/children that are the same age our children would have been.

  h. Needing to make major decisions, such as getting pregnant again, getting married again, moving, changing jobs, etc.

  i. Visiting the cemetery, purchasing a headstone, or deciding whether to scatter ashes and where.

  j. How to best honor our loved ones in special and meaningful ways.

  k. Feeling different and subsequently feeling isolated and/or just being sad.

  l. Being around other happy couples or families.

  m. Physical symptoms that arise from grieving, such as crying, irritability, impatience, lethargy, lack of motivation, depression, problems with sleeping, fast heartbeats, chest pain, weight gain, or loss of appetite.

Here are a few sample letters. You'll have to customize your letters, of course, so that they express your situation, including what you're going through and what you need:

Dear friends and family,

We want to share some of our feelings and suggest how you can help and support us. We have suffered a tremendous loss, and we need to grieve. Even though this may be uncomfortable for those around us, it's something we MUST do. As people may expect, we won't be over this in a few weeks. To heal, we have been told that we need to allow ourselves time to grieve; intense grief can last up to eighteen to twenty-four months. And even so, we know we will not be the same people we were before our loss.

We may need to talk about our situation and the details of our experience. We are suffering from broken hearts and shattered dreams. During this time, we need others to be there and listen to us, even if we have repeated our stories many times. This is the kindest thing you can do for us right now. We do not want to forget our loved ones and will need to mention them in the future. We would appreciate it if you would remember them, too, especially on difficult days, such as anniversaries, birthdays, Christmas, Mother's Day, and Father's Day.

Dealing with so many emotions at times can be overwhelming. We feel we are taking the steps we need to move through this time toward healing, peace, and hope for the future.

We plan to attend support group meetings. These meetings are a safe place to share our feelings with others who have faced similar situations. These meetings will not "fix" us quickly, but we hope they will offer us the tools to get through the first year of loss and beyond.

If we sound a little selfish, please understand. After we have healed and worked through our grief, we hope to be able to help others through similar situations so that what we have experienced will serve a purpose.

We are changed because of this situation and are sensitive not to criticize others for their choices in handling certain situations. Before our loss, we didn't understand the full impact of such a loss, so we wouldn't expect others to understand unless they have also been through something similar. We want to share this painful experience with you so you can understand our needs and potentially help others who need help and support in the future. No one will be able to take the pain away, but perhaps our experience will serve as a tool to help others in the future.

Thanks so much for your understanding and caring for us during this difficult time. You are truly loved and appreciated.

With much love,

Signature

Another example relating to sudden loss:

Dear friends and family,

I have recently suffered a devastating loss. I am struggling with things right now, and it may take time to work through this.

I wanted to let you know that I will cry from time to time. I don't apologize for my tears. They are not a sign of weakness or a lack of faith. They are a direct expression of love, sadness, and loss, but also, they are a sign of my healing.

At times, you may see me frustrated or anxious for no apparent reason. Many emotions are tied to grief that I never knew were connected, including envy, jealousy, frustration, fear, anger, helplessness, and more. All I know is that my emotions are intense right now because of my grief. Please be forgiving and patient if I don't always make sense to you. If I repeat myself, talk in circles, or go off on tangents, please know this is normal and all part of the grieving process. Sometimes, I feel like I am going crazy with all my emotions, but I'm assured this is normal.

More than anything else right now, I need your understanding and your presence. You won't always know what to say, and sometimes, it is just better not to say anything, but please, offer a phone call, text, touch, or a hug to let me know you care. Please don't wait for me to call you. Sometimes, it's hard to pick up the phone and make a call; conversely, please don't be offended if I don't answer your call. Just know I'm thankful you reached out and that you care. If I seem distant, please continue to pursue me. I may not be myself again for months; in fact, I will never be entirely the same. I will be forever changed because of this, but I know God will use this experience for good as He promises. I understand and trust that God is good and has a greater plan in all of this.

Please pray that I will see God working out the details in everything and for me to see the daily gifts God gives me to get me through each day. Please pray that I find meaning in my pain so that someday I will be able to use my pain to help others through theirs.

If you have experienced a similar loss, please feel free to share it with me. It helps to hear other people's stories. It gives me hope to know others have traveled a similar path and made it through. Don't be afraid to bring up the subject for fear of making me cry. It is healing to cry; if you should shed a tear or two, that is okay, too. There is something about sharing each other's sadness and heartbreak that is helpful, hopeful, and healing.

This loss is so excruciating right now. I have never experienced anything as devastating as this. To me, it seems the most painful thing I will ever experience. I cling to the knowledge that God is with me, and He will carry me through this time. With this faith and the care and love of family and friends, I know I will make it through this phase of life and experience joy again someday. I will be stronger for going through this. The most difficult times can help us grow and learn.

I'm so thankful for you, your love, and your care. Thank you for listening and praying and for helping me through this time. You are a gift for which I am forever thankful.

Much love,

Signature

Another letter sharing upcoming divorce:

Dear friend,

It is with much regret that I must share that my husband and I have separated. The divorce will be finalized in the next couple of months. We know this will be upsetting for our friends, but we also know this difficult decision is for the best for our family. The boys will live with me in an apartment near my work and the kids' school. I can be reached at _____.

I have always considered you one of my closest friends, so I wanted to let you know as soon as possible. I wanted to call you, but I just can't talk about it right now. I am getting professional help to work through this time. It isn't going to be easy for anyone, but we are slowly coming to terms with the changes.

As I know you are friends with our entire family, I hope we can stay close friends in the years to come.

I love you, my friend,

Signature

Other Things to Think about When Writing a Grief Letter

Don't worry about trying to include everything. If you think of additional things, you can write another letter later. Trying to anticipate everything you want to include will make the letter-writing more difficult. Speak from your heart and share the support you require from family and friends to make things easier as you grieve. Be sure to share your immediate needs. Grief evolves. A month or two later, you may have other needs. When different needs arise, you can create and send out another letter.

The people who genuinely love you will not be offended by your letter. If they are, then you probably need some distance from them for a while. Most will appreciate your letter and willingness to share openly and honestly what you need. It will take the guesswork away from them in trying to figure out how to deal with you and your situation.

If you don't tell people what you need, you risk being disappointed by loved ones and not being cared for in the way you would like. It takes courage to share your feelings, but once you do, you will feel a release, and those close to you will better know how to care for you to help you heal.

As you work through your time of loss, you will find that your loss not only affects you but also affects those around you. When people we love are hurting, we typically hurt for them, as we will discuss in the following chapter, "Everyone Grieves."

8:28

E

HOPE IN THE DARKNESS

CHAPTER 4

EVERYONE GRIEVES

Everyone is Terminal

"**E**veryone is terminal." This is a phrase I have heard many times over the years. Since this is true and everyone *is* terminal, it stands to reason that everyone will grieve at some point because everyone will experience loss. Grief is inevitable, and we will all experience it at various times throughout our lives. When we grieve the loss of someone or something we love, we are usually not alone in our grief; more often than not, those closest to us are also grieving.

This truth became a reality when I lost my first immediate adult family member, my beautiful sister, Darlene, when she was fifty-four. Darlene was seven years older than me and known as the "perfect child" in our family. Darlene was incredibly special and extremely smart. She graduated from Stanford University, where she met her husband and fell in love during a foreign exchange program in France. (Truly a fairy tale romance!) Once they graduated, they both received their MBAs from UCLA and landed excellent corporate jobs in New York City, promptly starting their family shortly after. Not only was Darlene brilliant, but she was also fun and funny. She made you feel like you were the most important and only person in the room when she talked with you. When their two children, Mark and Amy, started grade school, Darlene and Barry felt Manhattan wasn't the best place to raise their family, so they moved to a beautiful vintage home in Wayne, Pennsylvania. While Darlene was raising her family in Pennsylvania, I was raising mine in Southern California. We were on opposite coasts, yet we couldn't be closer. Although we were raised in a Christian home, she would say she didn't understand what it meant to be a Christian until later in life. Perhaps because of the age difference, it wasn't until we both married and started raising families that we started sharing thoughts and ideas about our faith, raising kids, and being a good wife, mother, and friend. At that point in our adult lives, we became not only sisters but dear friends and life support for one another.

I'll never forget the day when Darlene told me she had breast cancer. She was forty-eight. She called and told me she had to talk to me about something. It sounded serious, so I immediately stopped what I was doing and sat down on the stairs in my house. When she told me she had breast cancer, it didn't immediately hit me because I had limited knowledge and experience with breast cancer, thinking it was a type of cancer that seemed pretty common and easily treatable. No one in our family had ever been diagnosed with any kind of cancer before, so I just assumed she would probably have chemotherapy treatments and the cancer would most likely go away.

Unfortunately, Darlene's case was not typical. A lumpectomy showed that her cancer had metastasized and spread to other parts of her body. She endured many chemo and radiation treatments. Her body was terribly burned from the radiation treatments, which produced open wounds on her skin that wouldn't heal. She was in and out of doctors' offices and hospitals over the next six years. The amazing thing about Darlene was that she never seemed to complain about what she was going through. She fought an intense battle; throughout it, she was always more than willing to help and listen to other people and what they were going through. She never lost her sparkly eyes that let everyone know how special they were to her.

After six years of the cancer battle, her body couldn't fight any longer, and she passed away just a few days before Thanksgiving. We were all devastated. Everyone who knew her grieved her loss. Darlene's husband, children, our parents, brother, cousins, aunts, uncles, nieces, nephews, and friends were all grieving the loss of Darlene. My heart was breaking not only for the loss of my sister but for the collective grief, as well. I was especially heartbroken for my mom and dad because I could feel their loss more than most. We now shared the experience and understanding of child loss.

A mother or father losing their child is especially devastating for a few reasons. First, there is no other love like the love for your child. Secondly, because it is our greatest desire and natural instinct to protect our children from harm, we often feel we have failed them somehow when they die. And lastly, it is out of the usual order of things. Children are supposed to outlive their parents, not the other way around.

A couple of years before Darlene passed away and after she was diagnosed with breast cancer, my mom was also diagnosed with a different and very rare type of cancer. Darlene and my mom had been on a journey of cancer treatments, enduring many of the same things for several years alongside one another. I think Darlene's passing was just too much for my mom to handle, along with battling her own cancer, and within five months, my mother lost her battle with cancer, too.

With the loss of my sister and mother so close together, everyone was in shock. My dad lost his firstborn and his wife of nearly sixty years. My sister's children lost their mother and grandmother. My brother lost his sister and mother. My brother-in-law lost his wife, the mother of his children, and his mother-in-law. My kids lost their aunt and grandmother. When a child or spouse dies, the attention is typically directed toward the parent or surviving spouse, but there are usually many others affected by the loss who may feel left out. During times of loss, I encourage you to look beyond the immediate loved one who has had a loss and comfort others who are grieving, as well. Grandparents, siblings, aunts, uncles, cousins, and close friends also struggle with loss and suffer in their own way.

Men Grieve Differently

Additionally, consider how our society and culture place certain expectations on men. Although some men may appear strong and less affected, they are hurting just as much—possibly more. Women in grief tend to have more outlets to share their feelings and emotions, while men often feel invisible and isolated in their grief. After the loss of a child, caring friends or coworkers may come up to the father and ask how their wife or other children are doing with the loss, but rarely do they ask the father directly how he is coping. This is often true of other situations involving grief, such as when a man loses his job or is going through a divorce. The focus generally moves toward the wife or children and how they are doing, and the father is left to grieve and work through emotions and feelings alone.

When it comes to men in grief, unfortunately, there tends to be a different standard for men. It is a common misconception that men don't grieve. Men may turn to alcohol, anger, distancing, overworking, denying, or internalizing their emotions to work through their grief to preserve their manliness or manhood. However, these actions can become increasingly destructive and unhealthy when dealing with grief.

Our society somewhat understands women grieving because they share and show their feelings more often than men. Women have support systems. They tend to have more intimate friends they confide in, cry with, or share a cup of coffee, lunch, or glass of wine with, but for most men, the concept of intimacy and sharing is considered a weakness. Men fall into the stereotype of the "macho" male, who isn't allowed to grieve (as was shown in the example with Rick's boss in the previous chapter).

Men are not immune to grief and must express and work through it as women do. Some people believe it isn't considered "manly" to cry, and they think it is weak and unmanly to acknowledge the pain and sadness of loss, so men are at a distinct disadvantage when dealing with emotions of pain and loss. They have friends at work and maybe golf or drinking buddies, but those relationships are typically not intimate, where they share personal struggles, fears, sadness, and failures. Many men have friends they may have known their entire life, but they know very little about each other's personal lives or emotional struggles. When a male friend struggles, most men have no idea what to do to support them.

As a grieving woman, I *needed* to see my husband grieving the loss of our son, sister, and mom. I couldn't understand how Rick could get up and go to work each day as if everything were normal. I couldn't stop thinking about losing them, how much I wanted them with me, and how completely lost I felt. I questioned whether Rick missed them as much as I did. Not that I wished pain for my husband, but I needed to see that he was hurting to assure me that he loved and missed our loved ones as I did.

It wasn't until we received some grief counseling that I realized Rick was hurting just as much as I was, but he was trying to hide it from me to avoid upsetting me. He was trying to be strong and protect me, thinking he could "fix" the situation by hiding and suppressing his feelings. I learned through our counseling sessions that he often cried in his car to or from work or while taking our dog for a walk late at night. Through counseling, we learned to share our feelings and not hide anything. There were times when we were weak and times when we were strong. When one of us was having a particularly difficult time, the other was strong, and vice versa, so we could help one another with our weaknesses.

There were, however, a couple of occasions when we both had a hard time simultaneously. When this happened, we acknowledged our feelings, held each other, and cried together. Then, we would compose ourselves, maybe talk a little more about it, and continue our day. I remember one such time we were driving to visit some friends, and, on the way, we both became very emotional and just fell apart. Rick was driving and had to pull off the road because he couldn't see through his tears. We just sat in the car, held each other, and cried. I can't even remember what triggered our sadness. It could have been lyrics from a song we were listening to, something we were talking about, or something we saw on the drive; I'm not sure, but something hit us both at the same time. In those moments of sadness, often, there were no words. All we could do was hold each other with our thoughts and tears. After the tears finally stopped, we talked a bit and decided it was time to go, so we went on our way. It always felt good to have those crying moments. It was a release we needed, and afterward, we always felt stronger and ready to get through another day.

Although exhausting, there is usually a sense of relief and healing after having a good cry. Choosing the "no tears" or stiff upper lip approach will not work with grief. Emotions need to come out to work through grief healthily and truly get through it.

Kids Grieve, Too

Children and grief are deeply interconnected. Understanding how kids experience and cope with grief is crucial for supporting them during difficult times. Grief is the emotional response to a loss, and it can manifest differently in children compared to adults. They are often seen as resilient and ignorant of what is happening, so the attention they may need may not be given. Guilt, jealousy, and confusion can come into play with young children. They may feel guilty in thinking they did something to cause the situation. For young children, death and dying may not fully be understood, so they are confused about why they would be a big brother or sister one day and then find out they won't be one the next. Or why a parent, friend, grandparent, aunt, or uncle is no longer around. Jealousy and acting out may appear if the focus is now on someone or something else rather than on them. These feelings can stick with a child through adulthood if not addressed.

That being said, there are ways we can help children cope. With communication, patience, and love, most children will handle loss and adjust well.

Communication is the key. Explain the situation as much as possible, adjusting to the child's age and level of understanding. Children need simple information to adapt to the immediate changes in their lives and their future.

Allow children to ask questions and listen carefully to what they are asking. Respond simply, clearly, and truthfully with as much information as you feel they can handle for their age.

Encourage children to openly express their feelings. Assure them that crying, sadness, and other emotions are normal responses. It's alright for a child to see you cry. Be sure to talk to the child about your tears and reassure them that, even though you are sad, you are okay, and your sadness doesn't have anything to do with something they did. To relieve any additional burden, let them know it isn't their responsibility to make Mommy and Daddy feel better and that it is okay to cry when you feel sad.

Sometimes, words are not necessary. Offer your physical presence and affection. A comforting hug or touch to let them know you care and are available can be as powerful as words of comfort. (And that physical connection will also benefit you, too!)

Here are some additional tips for helping your children during times of loss:

⬧ **Accept their feelings** - Avoid telling a child how they should or should not be feeling. Try to accept whatever they may be feeling at that time.

⬧ **Share your feelings** - They will probably need to know how you are doing, even if they don't know how to ask.

⬧ **Be patient** - Children often need to ask the same questions repeatedly, so be patient with them in your responses.

⬧ **Maintain routines** - Security and stability are essential for children during times of tragedy and transition. Try to keep as many routines familiar to the child as possible and allow special times specifically for them.

⬧ **Quality time** - Schedule quality time with each child. Quality time can include being present. When your child needs attention, stop what you are doing, make eye contact, and listen.

⬧ **Give them some control** - Allow the child to make some of their own decisions about participating in family activities. It is helpful for children to feel they have some control and aren't forced into doing things they may not be ready for.

In some cases, children may benefit from professional counseling or therapy to help them cope with their grief, especially if they are struggling to adjust or if the loss has had a significant impact on their emotional well-being.

Remember that every child's grief experience is unique, and there is no right or wrong way to grieve. Providing a safe and supportive environment, along with patience and understanding, can make a significant difference in helping children navigate their grief journey.

Everyone Feels a Loss

It is important to be aware of the effects of loss on those around us, so we can be sensitive to others who may be indirectly involved. So many underlying emotions surface when loss and grief are experienced, and many people may be affected and struggle with situations that one may not expect.

I had an instance with a client who had a tough time after hearing about the loss of my babies. She was an older woman who had lost a child twenty years earlier and wasn't allowed to deal with her grief when she lost her baby. She had never been able to hold or see her baby. In those days, the loss of a baby wasn't talked about. After a loss, women were to act as if it had never happened and move on. It wasn't until I shared my story with her that her loss surfaced. It hit her hard and was an extremely emotional time for her. Hearing about my loss triggered intense emotions about her loss. This type of grief is known as delayed grief, where an individual isn't allowed or able to process the shock of loss when it occurs. Delayed grief can be triggered long after the initial loss. It is the reaction to unprocessed emotions, which can lead to both emotional and physical symptoms. Coping with delayed grief is similar to dealing with the typical emotions of initial grief. It is a matter of learning to address and manage feelings of sorrow at a later time.

I'm unsure whether she ever sought counseling to deal with her prior loss because I moved shortly after and never saw her again, but it has often made me think of the pain and grief she had buried for so many years. You just never know who will be affected by your story and situation.

In situations involving the loss of a child, grandparents often feel a double dose of pain, grief, and helplessness because they are not only grieving the loss of their grandchild, but as a parent, they are heartbroken to see their children in such pain. Grandparents whose children or grandchildren suffer from addictions may grieve the loss of quality time spent together and their hopes and dreams for the future; they may also experience guilt for somehow not doing enough to help or "fix" the situation.

Close friends suffer alongside those who are dealing with loss and grief. As the previous chapter discusses, friends often want to help but are simply at a loss about what they can do to help ease the pain. They, too, are grieving the loss and the lives they once had with their friends.

For example, a dear friend I had known since kindergarten was also expecting her first baby to be born shortly after Matthew's due date. I know the loss of Matthew was hard on her. It was difficult for her to see one of her dearest friends suffering such a loss while she was so excited about the arrival of her baby. I'm sure it was awkward for her to know how to support me while struggling with internal fears and excitement for her unborn child. We lived a few blocks from each other, and it was hard for us to be around one another for the rest of her pregnancy. All the hopes and dreams of our babies growing up together were lost. We wouldn't be able to enjoy learning about motherhood together as we had looked forward to since we were children. Losing Matthew was also a loss for my dear friend and others close to me.

I recently went to a memorial service for a friend's brother, who passed away suddenly at fifty-six. It is difficult to see someone hurting and in such shock of loss, especially when the person is close to you. No one truly understands the loss of a sibling unless they have experienced something similar. Her loss brought back so many memories of losing my close family members.

Grief is tricky because it continues to be triggered by particular memories or events later in life. Triggers can catch us completely off guard and can vary from person to person. What may be a trigger for one person may not affect another in the same way. Some common triggers include anniversaries, birthdays, holidays, locations, possessions, music, family events, milestones, and witnessing loss in others. It is essential to recognize these triggers as a normal part of the grieving process. Acknowledging and accepting the emotions they bring up can help individuals cope with grief more effectively.

My losses have given me the gift of empathy and being more sensitive to witnessing loss in others. This gift allows me to show grace to others, which is essential when someone is grieving. When I see someone hurting, I physically hurt, especially if they are experiencing loss. Before my losses, I wasn't very attuned to what others were experiencing because things generally came easy to me early in my life. Therefore, I did not understand the magnitude of grief that can accompany loss. After I experienced the loss of my son and subsequent family members, I became much more compassionate, sympathetic, and empathetic toward people. I could see more clearly how the simple daily duties of life seemed almost impossible at times and how grief continues through a lifetime.

I remember going to the store to get groceries or taking a package to the post office, and it felt so strange to be doing "normal" daily things and knowing that no one had a clue as to what I had just been through or was still going through. I realized then that I didn't know what others were going through, either. We never really know what a person's life is like on the other side of their Instagram or Facebook posts, or what the telemarketer on the other end of a phone call is genuinely experiencing, or what the person who cut us off in traffic during our commute to work is enduring.

Everyone is dealing with something and trying to make it through each day the best they can. Whether it is missing a loved one, struggling with paying the monthly mortgage, dealing with a cancer prognosis, worrying about children with addictions, grappling with a marriage that is falling apart, coping with mental illness, or just trying to make it day by day through a worldwide pandemic, everyone is hurting in some way.

After my initial loss, I began considering what everyone else was going through, so I tried to do what my mom instilled in me. She often said, "Try to put yourself in their shoes." It is excellent advice for us all. Doing so may soften our hearts and give us a better understanding of what someone else is thinking or feeling. As a result, it may make life a little more bearable and manageable for everyone.

Putting yourself in the other person's shoes goes hand in hand with the Golden Rule of treating others as you would want to be treated. Just as the Bible in Luke 6:31 states, "Do to others as you would like them to do to you." Don't you wish everyone would subscribe to this rule and behave accordingly? If we all made this a habit and treated everyone this way, we would live much more peaceful lives.

Your Grief Journey

We have used **Exercise 4** below in our support groups for many years to help people see and understand that they are grieving normally.

> *EXERCISE 4:* "Am I grieving normally?"
>
> People often ask three questions when going through grief:
>
> "Is this normal?"
>
> "Am I going crazy?"

"Will I ever get over this?"

A better question may be, "Is my grief healthy?" There is, of course, no one right way to grieve. It is quite normal to have many simultaneous emotions and thoughts while grieving. But even those who grieve healthily have times when they are overwhelmed by their grief.

The following checklist may help you figure out how you are doing. As time passes, you will find you will answer "yes" to more and more questions. This is a good exercise to do at various stages of your grief. Your answers will change over time, and you will be able to see your progress and realize that you are healthily moving through grief.

- Am I able to laugh without feeling guilty?

- Do I pay attention to my appearance (e.g., hair, clothes, make-up)?

- Do I enjoy being out with friends for an evening?

- Am I feeling pleasure in sexual experiences?

- Can I sit quietly by myself and think of things other than the loss?

- Do I take an interest in current events and news (e.g., television, radio, newspapers)?

- Am I able to do the daily tasks I'm used to performing (e.g., yard work, housework, cooking, and household maintenance)?

- Do I look forward to outings, trips, and special events?

- Am I involved in activities that I participated in before the loss (e.g., church work, volunteer work, clubs, sports teams, a job)?

- Can I talk about the loss without showing strong emotion (e.g., sadness, anger, jealousy)?

- Do I feel like the fog has lifted?

- Do I pay attention to my surroundings (e.g., beautiful scenery, the taste of food, the smell of perfume)?

- Can I get a good night's sleep and wake up feeling rested?

- Am I able to concentrate on work and conversation?

- Am I less forgetful and better able to think clearly?

- Can I recall past events? Can I remember happy or fun times I've experienced in the past?

- Do I feel stronger and more in control (e.g., less like I suffer from an open wound, better able to cope with other people's comments, and better able to cope with everyday crises)?
- Can I deal with everyday life without feeling panicked, frantic, or excessively worried (e.g., minor injury to a child, someone arriving late, or travel)?
- Do I feel that there is meaning to my life?
- Can I look back at what happened and feel that something good came out of the tragedy?

Again, there are no right or wrong answers here. This is just a guide to see where you are as you move through the grief journey. Be patient with yourself. Grief is a long journey. If you feel stuck and are not seeing progress or changes in any of your answers over the first year, it may be helpful for you to seek counseling to help you identify where you are "stuck" and allow you to move forward in your healing process.

REFERENCE B below is a "Grief and Loss Checklist" that can be helpful to take and review occasionally. Again, you can see that many emotions are associated with grief, and various physical symptoms, thoughts, and behaviors are often tied to grief and loss.

REFERENCE B

GRIEF AND LOSS CHECKLIST

Some Normal Grief Emotions

- ☐ Sadness
- ☐ Hurt
- ☐ Replaying Painful Memories
- ☐ Fear
- ☐ Misery
- ☐ Loneliness
- ☐ Shock
- ☐ Questioning
- ☐ Feeling overwhelmed

- ☐ Anxiety
- ☐ Regret
- ☐ Surprise
- ☐ Anger
- ☐ Numbness
- ☐ Disappointment
- ☐ Envy
- ☐ Indecisiveness
- ☐ Relief – of worry, of loved one from pain
- ☐ Frustration
- ☐ Self-blame
- ☐ Irritability

Some Normal Physical Symptoms During Grief

- ☐ Feeling dizzy or out of breath
- ☐ Having tightness in the chest or throat
- ☐ Being overly sensitive to noise
- ☐ Clenching the jaw or teeth, sore teeth
- ☐ Weak or tense muscles
- ☐ Pounding, racing pulses, or skipped heartbeats
- ☐ Feeling fragile or often on the edge of tears
- ☐ Feeling exhausted or lacking energy
- ☐ Dry mouth
- ☐ Headaches
- ☐ Panic attacks
- ☐ Feeling like there is a lump in your throat
- ☐ Feeling nauseous
- ☐ Difficulty sleeping

Some Normal Thoughts When Grieving

- ☐ Disbelief, thinking this can't be happening

☐ Blaming or anger at yourself, others, or God

☐ Being unable to concentrate

☐ Big reactions triggered by small things

☐ Obsession over the person who died or the situation of loss

☐ Feeling the presence of the person who died

☐ Feeling like you are going crazy with so many emotions swirling in your head

☐ Depression or sadness

☐ Fear of additional loss

☐ Confusion or memory loss

☐ Dreaming about the person who died or the situation of loss

☐ Questioning ("Why?" or "How Come?")

Some Normal Behaviors when Grieving

☐ Eating too little or too much

☐ Crying

☐ Social withdrawal

☐ Desire to talk about the person who died or the situation with anyone who will listen

☐ Being "absent-minded," disorganized, or forgetful

☐ Yawning or sighing more often

☐ Behaving restlessly or lethargically

☐ Socializing only with those in similar situations (people who "understand")

☐ Inability to sleep or restlessness

☐ Quick temper

☐ Apathetic behavior

Again, as mentioned in Chapter 2, the five stages of grief or loss (Denial, Bargaining, Anger, Depression/Despair, and Acceptance) may or may not be experienced in any particular sequence. It is essential to realize and address these stages as they arise so that you can understand that what you are experiencing are normal emotions of grief. With time, faith, and a better understanding of the emotions of grief, you will get to a place of acceptance and move toward the future with hope.

Myths and Realities About Grief

Grief is a normal response to any loss, not just the death of a loved one but any major event in our lives. Divorce, job change, and illnesses are all losses that can affect us profoundly.

Below are some common myths or misconceptions about grief and loss from the Hospice Foundation of America[14]:

Myth 1:   We only grieve deaths.

Reality: We grieve all losses.

Myth 2:   Only family members grieve.

Reality: All who are affected grieve.

Myth 3:   Grief is an emotional reaction.

Reality: Grief can affect people emotionally, physically, and spiritually.

Myth 4:   People should leave grieving at home.

Reality: We cannot always control where we grieve.

Myth 5:   We recover from grief slowly and predictably.

Reality: Recovering from grief is a non-linear process with no timeline.

Myth 6:   Grieving means letting go of the life we had before things changed.

Reality: We never fully let go of essential things in our lives.

Myth 7:   Grief finally ends.

Reality: Over time, most people learn to live with loss.

Myth 8:   People who are grieving are best left alone.

Reality: People who are grieving need opportunities to share their memories and grief and receive support accordingly.

The more we learn about grief and loss, the more we can be sympathetic and empathetic as others go through it. It would be so nice if people would begin to truly put into practice the Golden Rule and think about others and what they may be going through. Unfortunately, not everyone has the Golden Rule as their mindset. Often, people get angry and short-tempered when going through life's struggles. Anger is an emotion triggered by grief, hurt, fear, and loss of control, which is addressed in the next chapter.

8:28

HOPE IN THE DARKNESS

CHAPTER 5

I'M ANGRY

It's Okay to Be Angry

A nger is an emotion that God has given us. The question is, what should we do with our anger? What is the root of anger, and how can we manage it healthily?

Many people face anger in loss and grief: anger for not having more time with a loved one, anger at a spouse for having an affair, anger toward an employer for terminating a position, anger toward cancer, anger toward the person who died, for being left behind, anger at oneself for choices made, or anger at God for allowing a situation to happen. There are many reasons for anger in difficult circumstances, and though often justified, we need to learn how to best deal with and appropriately handle anger when it arises so that it doesn't hurt us or someone else.

The year after my mom and sister passed away was a blur of emotions. For a few years during their illness, I spent much time in Pennsylvania and Northern California, visiting and caring for them. When my mom was put on hospice care until she passed away, I stayed with her and my dad in Northern California. I was so thankful to have such a supportive husband to allow me that precious time with my parents during the last few months of my mom's life.

The night before I arrived, my dad had taken a fall and badly sprained his back, so I not only helped care for my mom but also for my dad. My dad's back was so bad that he couldn't lie down, so he ended up sleeping in the recliner chair in the family room while I slept with my mom in their bed. Although I felt bad that my dad had to sleep in the other room in a recliner, those weeks of sleeping with my mom in the same bed were priceless.

I'm not sure if it was the meds she was on or what it was, but it seemed that every night, usually at midnight and 3:00 AM, she would wake up and become chatty. I'm thankful that I don't need much sleep to function properly because there were a few nights when we never went back to sleep. We would just lay in bed and talk. It was that time together and those precious talks that I will forever remember and hold most dearly.

We talked about my mom's childhood and what it was like for her growing up on a farm in Manteca, California. We talked about how all the cousins used to ditch me while playing hide-and-seek in the alfalfa fields on Grandpa's farm. I was the youngest cousin, so no one wanted "little Karen" hanging around. We talked about my mom's sister, Pearl, who died at age ten, and how hard it was for her mom to deal with that loss. My Mom shared how she and my dad met and fell in love and how happy she was to have found someone like him to share her love and life with. She also shared how sad she was to leave him so soon and how very concerned she was about how Dad would be able to take care of himself after she was gone. Of course, I assured her I would make sure he was well taken care of.

We talked about faith and how important it is to have a solid foundation of faith on which to live your life and how she tried to show her faith to others by being a good example. She was never "preachy," but you always knew what she believed and could see God's love and peace shining through her.

We talked about my sister, Darlene, and how Mom would be with her soon in heaven. We talked about old boyfriends and prom dresses she made for me, family vacations, husbands, and raising our families. We even talked about sex and drugs. No subject was off-limits during those middle-of-the-night conversations.

We laughed and giggled a lot; sometimes, we just held each other and cried because we knew her time to leave was near. It was like having a slumber party with a best friend every night and wishing it would never end.

I had been told by the hospice nurse that sometimes, people need permission to let go, so I needed to tell my mom that it was okay to leave us, further assuring her that I would take care of Dad and that we would be okay. That was one of the hardest things I have ever had to do, but I know my mom needed that permission to take her last breath. Those weeks I stayed with my mom and dad are some I hold most dear to my heart.

My dad was distraught over losing his daughter and wife, so I felt it was my job to stay strong and keep everyone together. We arranged three memorial services: two for my sister (one in Pennsylvania and one in California for our West Coast friends and family), and one for my mom. All three services were beautiful, with many relatives and friends coming from around the country to honor and comfort our family. Through many tears, my dad and I rehearsed what he would say at the services—something neither of us ever thought we would have to do together. A few days after my mom's service, we decided to go through her things together and donated much of them to charity.

As much as my dad wanted me to stay longer, I knew I had to re-turn to Rick and the kids in Southern California and adjust to being a wife and mom again. I remember coming home and being emotionally exhausted. One of the first days after I came home, I found out that Rick had missed a deadline for an event Avery was to participate in. After finding out she wouldn't be allowed to participate, I completely lost it. I was home alone when I found out about the news and fell on the ground and cried. I'm usually quiet with my emotions, but I sobbed and yelled at God and Rick. I was angry at everything. I was angry with Rick for missing the deadline. I was angry that my mom and sister were no longer alive. I was angry that I couldn't call my mom and ask her for motherly advice. I was crushed and in intense grief over the losses and angry and frustrated with all of it!

After my outburst of emotions, I realized I was feeling anger and that this was part of my grieving process. I gathered myself together and started doing what I usually would at that time of day. It seemed so strange to just continue with life's duties. I started cooking, doing laun-dry, and working. I didn't know what else to do, so I started processing my grief just as we teach people to do in our grief support groups. I acknowledged my feelings when they came up and worked through the next year of grieving my sister and mom. **Just because I knew a lot about grief didn't mean I didn't have to go through it. I needed to experience the emotions of grief, including anger.**

During that following year, my father-in-law went in for routine surgery, and while in surgery, he died from heart complications. It was such a shock to us all, and once again, our family was hit with another loss. We couldn't understand how the doctors could have missed the possibility that my father-in-law's heart wouldn't be able to withstand the surgery. Once again, I was angry. Angry that our family had to endure so much loss and heartache.

Our Empty Arms sessions include an exercise where people think about and discuss how their family dealt with anger in their homes as they were growing up. It is an interesting exercise because we can look back and see the examples their parents set in their responses to anger and discuss whether we felt they handled a situation appropriately.

EXERCISE 5:

Feeling angry and placing blame is a natural and necessary part of accepting a loss. We can allow ourselves and others to become angry as we move from denial to acceptance.

Examine your current situation and write down who or what you may be angry with. Use the following three visual areas (God, others, and myself) to prompt writing down your thoughts.

I'm angry with _____ for _____

I'm angry with _____ for _____

I'm angry with _____ for _____

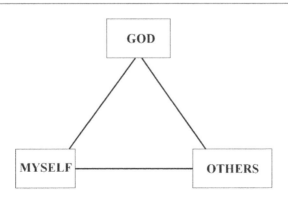

Questions to Consider

1. Anger with Others

- Is there anyone with whom you are angry, and why?
- How have you responded to your anger with others?
- How has your anger impacted your relationships?
- How do you feel your partner has responded to the situation?
- Explore any lingering resentment you may have been feeling.

2. Anger with Ourselves

- Is there guilt?
- What are you angry about when considering your role in the situation?
- Do you have issues with choices or decisions that were made?

3. Anger with God

When someone dies, our philosophical and spiritual foundations may be shaken. Often, we question the role God played in our loss and are very angry, believing He took something from us.

- What questions do you have for God?
- How will you find answers to your questions?
- Discuss the points you placed next to God on the chart.

Regrets: For the three areas, think about your "What if...?" questions, as well as the "Should have been" and "If only" statements and write them down.

_____

_____

_____

_____

_____

Hurt People Hurt People

It is helpful to know that the basis of anger is hurt and fear, so it makes sense that anger is a common emotion among people dealing with loss and grief. **Once we understand where the anger is coming from, we can address and deal with it in a healthy way.** We need to admit that we have been hurt or are afraid in situations of loss, including:

✧ Hurt as a result of the loss of a loved one.

✧ Fear of losing or not getting another job.

✧ Fear of death or dying.

✧ Hurt by the actions or reactions of others or ourselves.

Many of our basic human needs (food, shelter, love, identity, social affiliation, and security) are sometimes threatened after a loss, so it makes sense that grieving people, at some point, may become angry, causing them to lash out. Following a loss, there are typically significant changes one experiences, such as:

✧ Changes in family and friends and how they relate to us.

✧ A move to a different place.

✧ A change in financial or marital status.

Many changes may occur with loss where our basic needs are affected, leading to fear, hurt, and ultimately anger. Hurt people often hurt people. When we begin to feel angry, a good practice is to ask, "What am I feeling that is making me hurt or afraid?" The answer will often be that there has been some implied threat to one of our basic needs.

Being aware of our anger is the start of dealing with it, and being mindful when others are angry may help us understand them more appropriately. Do some self-examination and look inside or toward others to assess where the anger may be coming from. If you may have caused or directed anger toward someone else, an apology may need to be considered to work through the hurt and pain you have or may have caused, either directly or indirectly.

If you are the recipient of the anger, it may help to step back and think about what may be causing the other person to be hurt or afraid. What may have led them to anger? If we can come from a place of understanding anger (instead of reacting in self-defense or retaliation), we may be able to soften the situation by simply asking, "What did I do to deserve that?" The question may diffuse the anger, allowing them to think about it. Even if they answer, "I don't know," you've presented a challenge—to take a step back for reflection—and this can be helpful for all involved. This is also a great time to take Mom's advice of putting yourself in the other's shoes and using the Golden Rule of treating others how you would like to be treated.

When we are grieving (or involved with someone grieving), we should expect some level of anger. But if the anger seems intense or we don't feel we can manage it, the best option is to seek counsel from a therapist or pastor. If a friend or family member's anger seems uncontrollable and we don't feel we can ask for an explanation at that moment, we shouldn't take it personally. Knowing that anger is a natural part of grief can help us work through our suffering and help others, ultimately leading to additional healing.

Knowing the connection between anger and grief helps us understand why we may feel or behave as we do. Not allowing others—or ourselves—to go through anger may slow down the grief process and hinder progress. No one wants to stay in anger, so it is best to identify it, address it, deal with it, and move through it. We need to trust ourselves and the grief process. We won't stay in it forever, but we may need to get angry at times as we work through our grief toward acceptance and hope for the future.

As we work through the various emotions caused by grief, there may be times when there is a sense of numbness or feeling tired of "feeling." We can become numb to feelings, desires, and things that once were important but now seem unimportant. The following chapter examines how numbness can be a part of the journey out of the darkness.

8:28

N

HOPE **IN** THE DARKNESS

CHAPTER 6

NUMBNESS

Numb With No More Tears to Cry

Shortly after losing my father-in-law, my picture-of-health brother, Terry, was diagnosed with rare bone cancer on his sacrum (the area at the base of the lumbar vertebra). Terry underwent chemo treatments and radical surgeries on his spine, which left him unable to do many of the things he had loved to do his entire life.

Terry was an outdoorsman and loved skiing, hiking, biking, camping, traveling, and adventures. As a landscape architect, he worked on projects and loved building things. He was diagnosed with cancer just two years after he married the love of his life, Erika. They met while skiing in Tahoe and fell instantly and madly in love. I had never seen my brother happier! Shortly after my brother's cancer diagnosis, my dad was diagnosed with two types of lymphoma cancers (one slow-growing and one more rapid). It felt like déjà vu—just like the women in my life, Terry and my dad were battling cancer and dealing with chemo treatments simultaneously.

During the following year, there were many cancer treatments, visits to doctors and hospitals, surgeries, and clinical trials; we made trips back and forth between southern California and northern California to visit whenever we could.

Yet during that time, another devastating loss hit us. Rick's mom was diagnosed with Parkinson's disease and Chronic Obstructive Pulmonary Disease (COPD) while living in San Diego with his sister, who had been helping take care of her since Rick's dad passed. She experienced a painful fall at the house and the stress and trauma of the fall, combined with the recent loss of her husband, caused her to contract a severe case of shingles. She was in excruciating pain and on hospice care for weeks. At one point, she told me how tired she was. The two of us had a special relationship, and I remember my last conversation with her. As I told my mom, I told my mother-in-law it was okay to let go if she was tired and didn't want to fight anymore. We told each other how much we loved and appreciated each other as "moms." A few days later, she took her last breath in the arms of my husband and one of her grandsons. She, indeed, was a wonderful mom, grandmother, and mother-in-law. This was now another significant loss for our family.

Soon after the loss of Rick's mom, cancer spread to other parts of my brother's body, and his once-strong body couldn't fight any longer. I remember sitting with him in the hospital when he told me he didn't think he could fight cancer any longer. The cancer spread to his esophagus, so he could no longer eat or drink. He loved good food and wine, and the thought of never sharing a meal and a glass of wine again with his beautiful wife hit him hard. He admitted to me that he wanted to go home, so we arranged hospice care for him so he could be in his comfortable home with Erika and their dog, Jazzmin.

Terry didn't like people being sad, so he always attempted to "lighten things up." The final and most significant example of this was on Halloween. He had been home from the hospital for about a week, and friends and family stopped by all day to see him. He was surrounded by people he loved dearly. He also loved Jack Daniel's Whiskey, so even though Terry could barely swallow, he wanted to have a couple of shots of JD with his friends.

It was such a surreal day and night. He was set up in a hospital bed in the living room, barely able to move. Every few minutes, the doorbell rang with a group of kids yelling, "Trick or treat!" Terry wore a goofy turkey hat throughout the day, and I wore an orange and black polka-dot witch's hat. At one point, it was just Terry and me alone together, and he asked me to promise to ensure Erika was taken care of when he was gone. Once again, I gave a loved one assurance and permission to let go. We cried together, and he promised he would see me again in heaven.

Shortly after, Erika and some of his friends returned to the room, and we all noticed Terry's breathing had changed. We knew he didn't have much time left. It was a very somber scene with us sitting by his bed, either holding his hands or being draped over him crying when Terry suddenly lifted his head and said, "Trick or Treat!" Of course, we all started laughing amid our tears because it was just like Terry to lighten things up. "Trick or Treat" were Terry's last words before taking his last breath that Halloween night.

Once again, our family was thrown into a time of intense grief. I felt as though I would never be able to escape my intense emotions and feelings, but then there were other times when I was just too tired to feel. I was numb.

To move out of the darkness of loss and grief, you need to continue taking steps toward healing and gaining hope for the future. However, there may be times when you just don't feel like doing it anymore. It's just too hard and takes so long. Grief is certainly exhausting. There will be times when you feel like you are on an emotional roller coaster and can't wait to get off, but in the middle of the emotional twists and turns, surprisingly, you may suddenly feel nothing.

Often, after a loss, there is a period of numbness, and you stop feeling emotions completely. Things don't seem important anymore. Feelings of listlessness, indifference, disinterest, and general lack of concern become a daily occurrence. The things we used to enjoy now seem unfulfilling and unimportant. It is difficult to be motivated to do anything, including grieving. Previously, you may have been crying every day, but then comes a numbness, and you feel like you have no more tears to cry or feelings to feel.

The feeling that you have nothing to contribute—or that you can't relate to the feelings and emotions of others around you—can be a scary and lonely place. The absence of emotions can be just as painful or stressful as feeling too many. Major depression can occur because of apathy ("what is the point of anything"), particularly when you feel numb to everything around you.

Emotional numbness can be extremely disturbing, especially after a loss when you expect to feel so much. After a loss, for example, others may be highly emotional and in touch with their feelings when you haven't been able to shed a tear. So, you may wonder, *What is wrong with me? Did I not love them as much as I should?* or *Why don't I feel anything?*

Numbness during grief is alienating because you know you should be sad about the loss, but you can't access any feelings; you are left feeling isolated and estranged from others around you who are more visibly grieving the loss.

Types of Numbness

Some examples of numbness in grief include the following:

1. ***When there are no more tears to cry***: For some, numbness comes when there are no more tears. You have gone through so many grief emotions that there's nothing left to feel but numbness.

   When we experience intense grief, there is comfort in knowing that the tears result from our love for the person who died. If those tears and emotions stop, a sense of emptiness can result, and perhaps uncertainty. As difficult and painful as the intense feelings of grief can be, those emotions are strangely something to hang on to and rely upon. When no tears are left, we can find ourselves a little lost about what to do next. After crying every day for nearly six months, I remember a day when I didn't cry. It was such a strange and unfamiliar feeling! As time went on and with more healing, I began to have more days without tears than with tears. For me, that was a comforting sign that I was healing and moving forward.

2. ***Numbness to avoid guilt:*** This can be hard to understand. To ease the guilt of moving forward without the person we lost or about being happy again, we sometimes avoid our emotions, stuffing them deep down. We try to escape certain feelings that make us feel guilty. After grieving for a long time and finding that our emotions have come to a halt, it may feel inappropriate to have feelings of joy or laughter again; you feel guilty for having fun, laughing, or enjoying yourself. This, too, is normal. When you are ready, try to allow yourself to feel joy and happiness as welcomed signs of strength and recovery.

3. ***Numbness toward activities once enjoyed:*** This is common for people who experience a loss, especially in the beginning. After

a loss, perspectives change; things that once seemed important no longer bring the same joy, excitement, fulfillment, satisfaction, peace, or fun. This loss of desire or interest for what once brought joy can feel like numbness—you can't get excited about anything anymore. This additional loss can make you feel like you have lost a part of yourself and who you once were.

4. *Numbness because nothing matters:* This isn't the same as losing interest in activities. It is more like losing interest in the world around us in general. This is a numbness toward other people, including their problems and concerns, but also toward the problems and concerns that once filled our lives. Finances, obligations, schedules, work, political issues, and community are unimportant. There are feelings of *What's the point? Does anything matter?* and *Who cares?* Perspectives on life, God, politics, and the world are changed. As a result of the loss, nothing seems to matter. Major depression can sink in with this type of numbness. It becomes too much to do simple daily tasks, such as getting out of bed, getting dressed, eating, and going to work. Hopelessness and defeat can leave someone with no desire to do anything. This is dangerous. Get in touch with a professional if you feel hopeless and lack the purpose to move forward and live life. Here are some free resources:

✧ Call 2-1-1 to talk with a resource specialist for free to find resources in your area.

✧ Text 741741 to reach a crisis counselor.

✧ Call 988 for the suicide and crisis lifeline

5. *Numbness as self-preservation:* This may be more of a choice or decision than some other examples of numbness. Since the emotions of grief are painful, some people decide (or at least try) to never subject themselves to loss or grief again. They push love away and put up protective walls, trying to guard their hearts by choosing not to love. People who open their hearts to love can have their hearts broken again if that love isn't reciprocated, so some people just quit trying for fear of failure, rejection, and heartbreak. Some people will do everything possible to keep a relationship superficial and harden their hearts against deeper relationships to avoid heartbreak. For example, someone who has lost a job recently may

find it difficult or impossible to muster the confidence to try to get another job for fear of rejection and loss again *(Why even try?)*. They are paralyzed and do nothing for fear of defeat. Ironically, in such situations, defeat is the outcome.

Some Personal Numbness Experiences

I remember going to the mall with my mom a few months after losing my son. Everyone seemed to be going along and living happy lives. I remember feeling like the world was moving ahead, and I was simply watching it.

I was numb. There were no more tears to cry, no laughter, no desire to shop at the mall, no desire to do anything. I remember being in the car in the parking garage with my mom and just sitting there staring. I didn't get out of the car. I didn't want to go shopping as I usually would. I was just sitting there. My mom pulled me close to her like she did when I was a little girl. She wrapped her arms around me, and we just held each other. I appreciated her doing that because she comforted me in a way no one else could. It was such a simple act, but one only a mother could do. We didn't talk because, in those moments of embrace, nothing could be said that hadn't been said already. After some time, I remember telling her I just felt numb. All I could say to her was that I thought the whole situation was sad and that I felt empty.

An instance of "numbness to avoid guilt" occurred after a doctor's visit when, after being poked, examined, tested, and having to make tough decisions, I remember saying something to Rick about one of the doctors that made us both start laughing. But we quickly stopped because it seemed inappropriate for us to laugh during such a sad time. It felt good to laugh, yet strange. We felt guilty. The conflicting emotions caused us to push both sadness and laughter away—and we were left with nothing.

Slowly, we allowed ourselves to laugh and experience joy again. Still, it took time to understand that we didn't need to feel guilty for experiencing laughter and having pleasant emotions. We realized it was okay and good to laugh instead of always being sad.

Resolving Numbness

So, how do we get out of the numbness? No one wants to stay in a place of feeling nothing. It is a terrible place to be. God gave us feelings and emotions, and it is unnatural to avoid them. Most people want to move away from this phase as quickly as possible but moving out of numbness just because you want to is hard. It requires strength and will. Fortunately, there are some things you can do to work through it. First, numbness must be recognized as a part of grief. You must acknowledge that it won't last forever. With time and perseverance, you will get through it.

But these things I plan won't happen right away. Slowly, steadily, surely,
the time approaches when the vision will be fulfilled. If it seems slow,
do not despair, for these things will surely come to pass. Just be patient!
They will not be overdue a single day! Habakkuk 2:3 (TLB)

If you find yourself or someone you love feeling so numb that they are considering harming themselves, seek professional help to guide them.

REFERENCE C below ("Mental Health Evaluation") is an assessment tool to help determine whether you are moving toward hope and healing. Refer to it occasionally to assess and manage your emotional state throughout your loss.

REFERENCE C lists nine simple questions you can ask yourself or a loved one to help recognize a developing mental health or addiction problem before it reaches a crisis. As with any such screening, there will be some false positives. Not every chest pain is a heart attack, and not every unusual emotional state or thought pattern indicates mental illness. That said, you should not simply ignore persistent chest pains or persistent changes in your mental or emotional state. Follow up with your family physician for further evaluation if indicated.

REFERENCE C

REFERENCE C

MENTAL WELLNESS SELF-ASSESSMENT TOOL

INSTRUCTIONS: Check the box that most closely applies.

State of Mind	ALWAYS OR NEARLY ALWAYS	OFTEN	SOME-TIMES	NEV-ER OR NEARLY NEVER
1) I feel emotionally numb.				
2) I wish I could just cease to exist.				
3) I think others would be better off without me.				
4) I lose my temper or over-react to small things and then feel bad about how I have treated people.				
5) I feel I need a drink or some other drug to make it through the day or sleep at night.				
6) I experience thoughts or voices that I cannot get out of my head.				
7) I think people are out to get me.				
8) I have feelings of impend-ing doom.				
9) I feel pretty good about my life and the future.				

Here's what your answers mean:

Having some of these thoughts occasionally does not mean something is wrong with you. Everyone has them sometimes. However, the first eight mental and emotional states listed are generally rare in healthy individuals. Experiencing any of these mental states often or sometimes may indicate you are moving toward a mental health problem or addiction. In contrast, feeling "pretty good" about one's life is more or less the "default setting." The absence of this mildly positive emotional state implies you are experiencing more stress than you can tolerate. See further explanations below.

State of Mind #1: *"I feel emotionally numb."*

Clinical depression is not the same thing as sadness. Depression is the absence of an ability to experience positive emotions like love, joy, or contentment. The earliest and most persistent symptom of clinical depression is often a kind of painful emotional numbness, as discussed earlier. That is, it is the inability to enjoy even the small moments of pleasure daily: eating a favorite meal, finding a good parking spot, or getting a hug from your kid. Emotional numbness is rare in people not experiencing depression but very common in those with depression. Even individuals experiencing profound grief can usually muster some happiness over the outpourings of support from friends and family, but perhaps not if they are experiencing depression.

State of Mind #2: *"I wish I could just cease to exist."*

Even when a person is experiencing significant emotional distress, thoughts about suicide are rare; instead, the person just wants the pain to stop. So, a feeling that one would like to just cease to exist suggests that the present condition may not run its course on its own. It's as if your unconscious brain does not believe that your body will be able to fix the problem without outside help. Even people who have suffered mild seasonal depression in the past are not prepared for this much more serious state of depression.

State of Mind #3: *"I think others would be better off without me."*

First, if you think this way, you are almost definitely wrong. The loss of a loved one, particularly if people feel that they are somehow at fault in some way (perhaps by failing to show how much the loved one was wanted and needed), causes tremendous emotional pain. Believing others would be better off without you suggests a turn towards severe depression.

ANALYSIS OF STATE OF MINDS 1, 2, AND 3

If you have been experiencing all three of these mental states, you may be heading toward a major state of depression. Individually, they are red flags for depression; when they occur together, they raise even more serious concerns.

State of Mind #4: *"I lose my temper or overreact to small things and then feel bad about how I have treated people."*

Mild traumatic brain injury or exposure to high levels of stress hormones can impair the functioning of the part of the brain that calibrates emotions. This causes emotions to easily swing to extremes. Mild annoyances can trigger rage, and minor disappointments can plunge the person into despair. This emotional instability is the signature symptom of Post-Traumatic Stress Disorder (PTSD). Only a small percentage of patients with PTSD have flashbacks, but nearly everyone with PTSD reports emotional instability and difficulty with personal relationships. If you find this happening to you, you may want to find ways to reduce your stress hormone levels and monitor and consciously regulate your emotional responses. Remember that whether a person experiences PTSD is not dependent on how much stress they have objectively experienced, but rather how much cortisol and other stress hormones their bodies have produced in response to that stress. Like an allergic reaction, some people will overproduce stress hormones in response to specific pressures that otherwise may not affect others so drastically.

State of Mind #5: *"I feel I need a drink or some other drug to make it through the day or to get to sleep at night."*

Addiction is not a matter of how much alcohol or other drugs you use or how frequently. Addiction is the process of your body adapting to the presence of a drug in a way that makes it progressively less effective over time, which makes it difficult for your systems to function correctly without it. The feeling that using the drug is a matter of need is often the first warning signal that drug use is becoming drug dependence.

State of Mind #6: *"I experience thoughts or voices that I cannot get out of my head."*

If a person hallucinates, they usually cannot identify it as a hallucination. In fact, most people who experience hallucinations believe they are real. Moreover, flashbacks often seem like memories, and obsessions seem like a highly focused concern. In these circumstances, however, the thoughts or voices are not wanted and continue even if the person tries to shut them out. Frequently experiencing thoughts or voices in your head that you cannot shut out suggests you are losing control over the direction of your mind. If you are experiencing this, you should seek help immediately.

State of Mind #7: *"I think people are out to get me."*

Few people probably wish you ill, unless you are in a witness protection program. It could be paranoia if you start thinking people generally have hostile intentions toward you. Even people who receive death threats from anonymous Twitter trolls probably do not always think about those threats, and they probably do not generalize their fears to include everyone around them, either.

State of Mind #8: *"I have a feeling of impending doom."*

Before suffering a major heart attack, many patients reported that they had been experiencing a feeling of impending doom for days or weeks before the episode. Pregnant women have shared similar experiences shortly before a miscarriage, as well as people with various mental health diagnoses before a first psychotic episode. When the parts of your brain that unconsciously monitor the functioning of various organs detect a severe problem, they try to warn the conscious mind in the only way available to them: through emotions. A feeling of impending doom is the most serious warning message your unconscious brain can send you. In essence, your brain thinks whatever problem develops could kill you. Maybe your immune system is losing a battle with an infection, your heart muscle is not getting enough oxygen, or one or more neurotransmitter levels in your brain drop to levels preventing critical circuits from functioning. If so, this is a sign to contact your physician.

State of Mind #9: *"I feel pretty good about my life and the future."*

The default emotional setting for the human mind is mildly optimistic. Not everything is great and wonderful, but things are okay, pretty good, or fine. As in, *Maybe I am going through a rough patch now, but I have a roof over my head and enough to eat.* Or if not that, then *I have my health* or *I have good friends and people who care about me.* Or at least you may think, *I hope my situation will improve.* People vary greatly in their life circumstances and general optimism or pessimism. However, no matter what they are going through now or have experienced in the past, their brains still keep trying to pull them back to a baseline mental state with strong survival value. Feeling pretty good about life allows people to strive for improvements without getting too discouraged about setbacks. Suppose a person does not regularly have at least this mildly positive worldview. In that case, it indicates that the stress they are experiencing (financial, physical, or emotional) exceeds their ability to tolerate it. Such a person should seek help either to reduce some of the sources of stress in their lives or to develop better stress management skills because their unconscious mind is giving up on them.

Again, below are additional resources for immediate help.

✧ AmericanMentalWellness.org info@AmericanMentalWellness.org

✧ Call 2-1-1 to find resources in your area.

✧ Call 988 Suicide & Crisis Lifeline.

✧ Crisis Text Line - Text 741741 to be connected with professionals who can help.

✧ Mental Health America for additional online Mental Health Tests https://screening.mhanational.org/screening-tools/

The next chapter will take a personal inventory and look at productive ways to work through numbness, grief, and loss. Finding a manageable and healthy way to move from the darkness of grief and loss toward light helps you continue to heal and provides hope for the future.

8:28

T

HOPE IN **T**HE DARKNESS

CHAPTER 7

TAKE A PERSONAL INVENTORY

How Am I Doing?

After spending time in the darkness, living through periods of numbness, or just trying to grasp all the emotions involved with grief and loss, a time will come when you simply want to move forward and feel better again. No one wants grief to stay with them forever, but it can easily take a year or more to work through the heaviest grief healthily. Grief is a day-by-day and moment-by-moment journey, so this chapter provides some grief survival guidelines that may prove helpful in moving toward hope and peace in the future.

A personal inventory can help you understand where and how you move forward. Whether it has been days, weeks, months, or years, reviewing the guidelines below is a good idea to check in with yourself to ensure you are exercising self-care. Another way to check on your progress is to read your story from Chapter 2 to see whether anything has changed; if you haven't already, you may want to share your story with someone. There is healing each time you can share your story out loud with someone.

Below are some guidelines for creating a healthier lifestyle along your healing journey, including questions you can ask yourself.

GRIEF SURVIVAL GUIDELINES

Self-Care

Are you getting adequate rest, nutrition, and exercise? These are basic needs that will benefit you in your healing. Exercise daily, and do something to get yourself moving, even if it is a walk around the block. Take note of these things and make sure you are taking care of your health. Diet, exercise, and sleep are critical to mental health.

Drink Fluids

Drink plenty of liquids (preferably water) per day. Avoid caffeine, alcohol, and soda, or have them in moderation.

Take One Day at a Time

Don't think too far ahead. Break the day down into manageable parts if the whole day seems too overwhelming. Set small goals so that each goal met becomes an accomplishment to give you the incentive to make it to the next, however small it may be. For example, the plan may just be getting out of bed and making it, or getting out of bed, making your bed, and then making breakfast for yourself. Be sure to set your own goals, not ones that others may set or place on you.

Read and Learn

Learn as much as you can about grief and the healing process. This will give you a better understanding so that you can overcome some of your fears. Often, a lack of information about the emotions involved with grief and loss makes things feel so much worse when grieving.

Listen to Music

Music can be therapeutic, especially during a period of grief and loss. There may be songs that bring emotions to the surface each time you listen, which is okay. There were songs I often played during my darkest moments because they brought me comfort. Some of them will always bring me to tears. The songs I listened to included words that expressed exactly how I felt and provided comfort and hope. It is helpful to know that others think some of the same things, so we don't feel so alone.

Get Away

Take a break and get away for a few days if possible. Plan a trip to experience a new environment. This was one of the best things Rick and I did for ourselves. We planned a trip to a B&B in the Napa area and escaped for a few days. We found a remote place in the woods without phones, computers, or TV. The couple who ran the B&B brought us meals so we could eat whenever we wanted; we could come and go as we pleased. It was very private. We took long walks and enjoyed the outdoors and the lazy dog that lived there.

Most importantly, we just enjoyed being together. We had long talks yet were sometimes silent; getting away and doing something different for a few days was good. If time or money is an issue, a trip to the beach to sit on the sand or a drive to the mountains or lake to experience a change of scenery can be refreshing for your soul.

Daily Affirmations

Give yourself a positive phrase or word to repeat each day. Acknowledge that you will not always feel as you do. Trust that healing takes time. It takes much more time than you would like it to. As much as I didn't want to hear it then, the saying is true that time heals. That being said, you will never be fully healed. Your grief will never entirely go away because your love for what or whom you lost will never disappear entirely, but time does allow for healing and can change perspectives. Daily affirmation helped me focus on one thing each day, which helped me gradually move forward in my healing.

Write

When experts suggest journaling or another form of writing, the most common response is, "But I'm not a writer!" or "My writing isn't any good." Keeping a journal or recording your thoughts in a diary isn't about writing something perfectly; it's about getting your thoughts and feelings out. Write letters, notes, or poems about your loss. Use prompts to get your ideas flowing, or just start writing whatever comes to mind. Studies show that journaling provides an emotional release, which seems to lower stress, reduce anxiety, and promote better sleep. Journaling also provides an avenue for self-expression, all while increasing awareness of yourself and others.

I was introduced to a technique called "response writing," which I found very helpful. I learned it through a long-time friend, Rechelle, who lost her three-month-old infant son, Christian. Rechelle recorded her grief through response writing for an entire year. She started each day by writing a letter or prayer addressed to her son, God, Jesus, or the Holy Spirit, and then she waited in silence for a response. As soon as she was given thoughts, she immediately wrote down the answer she was given. This process is similar to the *Jesus Calling* books by Sarah Young, in which she prays, is attentive, and listens to what she feels God is trying to reveal to her through Jesus' words and Bible verses.

This experience was truly amazing when I tried it. The responses I received were often surprising because they were not typically how I would talk or write. I truly believe these responses were God-inspired because they were always words of truth, hope, and comfort; they were exactly what I needed to hear from my heavenly Father at the time. Below are some excerpts from Rechelle Conde-Nau's book, *Standing Tall*, so you can see how response writing can be a powerful and healing exercise. You will also read more about Rechelle and her story in Chapter 16, "Stories of Survival and Hope."

January 10, 1998 – (two weeks after their infant son, Christian, died in Rechelle's arms.)

> *Dear God,*
>
> *So many questions. So much pain. And yet some relief and understanding. There is some peace. I wish I understood and knew more. I hunger for the answers; I thirst for knowledge.*
>
> *My boy is gone, and I ache as I have never ached before. For the first time, I look forward to death to be with him again.*
>
> *I am so proud of all that Christian is about, so honored to be his mother, and no, Lord, I wouldn't change being his mother, wouldn't change Your plan. He did so much. I want to continue his legacy after some healing.*

How do you heal? Lord, I couldn't do this without You. I feel I need stronger guidance. Please point me in the right direction.

Hold me. Wipe away my tears.

Your loving child,

Rechelle

Response:

Dear Rechelle,

You have so many of the answers. There is no substitute for going through it. It is work, remember how short this time is compared to eternity.

I have sent you many messages. They come in all forms. Listen. Listen to learn.

There will be comfort. There will be joy again. I love your son as I love you.

I promise you will be together again.

Your Father

April 13, 1998 (four months after loss)

My dearest Lord,

You did so much for us. I am continually amazed by You and Your love for me. I am ashamed of any doubts I've had, of any fear I've felt. I think my mourning has rendered me raw, but on the other hand, it has caused me to be hungry and open to You in a way I hadn't been before. I have always loved You but I didn't understand until Christian how much, or that You must, You do, come first.

Thank you for my family, our dog, Lacey, prayer, Your / word, and my beloved Christian.

Love, Rechelle

Response:

Dear Rechelle,

To be grateful is a wondrous thing. Try to find thanks in all situations, even when the opposite would seem to be true, For I am there in all times.

Give the glory to the Father, for through Me, He is there.

Love, Jesus, the Son

May 30, 1998 (five months after loss)

Dear Lord,

Why am I feeling so discouraged and down? Is this part of my grief or something else? At any rate, it doesn't feel so good but I am trying not to be so hard on myself. I think I'm entitled to some crummy moments.

Help me to stay focused on You. Bring me Your blessings, especially of knowledge in Your truth.

Love, Rechelle

Response:

Dear Rechelle,

It's okay to feel down sometimes. I did too. Focus on the Father, bring it to Him and He will help you heal. It does take time and it does go back and forth. Remember that I know both the intentions of your heart and your desires too. Remember how much I love you. And you are worthy.

Love, Jesus

September 7, 1998 (nine months after loss)

Dear Lord,

A good beginning to my day — wonderful reading, sincere prayer, you are so awesome. I don't often understand the rhyme or reason to things sometimes but I know if I hang in there and trust You, it always works out. Always.

Thank You for Your love.

Love, Rechelle

Response:

Dear Rechelle,

You will know great love as you do now. Remember to give more than you get okay? Don't question it. Just do it.

Love, Jesus

Whether you try this type of response writing or not, I hope that you will at least attempt to write or journal regularly in one way or another. Journaling is an excellent way to free up your mind and get your thoughts down on paper. Always date your writing because, over time, when you reread some of your journal entries, you will be able to see how far you have come from where you once were, affirming the notion that healing is, in fact, possible.

Accept Help

When people offer to help, say, "Yes!" People want to help, so allow them to do so. If someone wants to bring you a meal, say, "Yes!" It makes them feel like they are doing something to offer support in the situation, and it is beneficial for you not to worry about cooking. You need to eat, so allow others to take care of you. If they offer to pick up groceries, do your laundry, or mow your lawn, say, "Yes!" And if they ask you whether you need help with anything, but don't offer anything in particular, say, "Yes!" and give them a specific task with which you could use help.

Say, "No"

As important as it is to say "Yes!" to people who offer help, it is also okay to say "No!" to doing things you don't want to do. If you are invited to a baby shower or a social gathering, and you know you aren't ready for that yet, it is okay to say, "No." If someone invites you to go somewhere and you don't feel prepared to do it yet, it is okay to say, "No." Do what you think you can or want to do. It is okay to bow out of things you aren't ready for, especially holiday events.

Holidays can be especially challenging because the feelings of loss during a special holiday may be accentuated. Holidays typically involve family, which can be wonderful, but some family dynamics can also be complex. There may be sadness, jealousy, or envy in being around siblings, cousins, or grandchildren. As wonderful as holidays can be in terms of being surrounded by family, they can also bring pain and sorrow. If you know that being around certain people or activities will be too much for you to handle, it is okay to say, "No." The people who know you will still love you and should understand that you aren't ready to do certain things yet. (And even if they don't quite understand, those who will stand by you will extend the grace you're asking for.)

Don't Rush into Major Decisions

Give yourself time before making big decisions. In fact, if you can, don't make any significant decisions for the first year after the loss. If a decision needs to be made immediately, make it carefully. Ask a trusted friend or family member for assurance about the decision and whether it seems reasonable to them. Until you have had time to heal, try to delay any significant decisions, such as buying a new house, changing jobs, getting pregnant, or adopting a pet.

Stay Close to Family and Friends

Surround yourself with "safe" friends and family members—people with whom you can freely share your feelings. Spend time with those who can understand your grief and emotions as best as they can. Spend time with friends and family who will listen without judgment and avoid offering possibly unwelcome opinions about how you should be grieving.

We were lucky to have a wonderful group of friends and family to share and spend time with regularly. It was nice to have friends we could call at the last minute to get together and play a game or just talk, cry, or provide a listening ear whenever we needed it. I am forever grateful for the close friends and family members who have helped me through my darkest and most difficult times.

Pamper Yourself

Allow yourself to take care of *you*. Treat yourself to something just for you. Go to the movies, read a good book, buy something new for yourself, take a bubble bath, get a manicure, treat yourself to ice cream, take a trip to someplace you've always wanted to see, or have a nice meal out. It is time to prioritize yourself because you are special, you deserve it, and self-care is so important. You need to be loved and cared for now, especially by *you*.

Create Alone Time

Take time to be alone with your thoughts (as hard as it may be). Think about what has happened and what steps to take to let you move forward with a fulfilling life. Provide yourself time to grieve. Allowing yourself the time to be alone and in your feelings and thoughts entirely is another form of self-care and can go a long way in your healing.

Acknowledge Your Emotions

Don't stuff or hide your emotions. Be honest with yourself and lean into them. Allow yourself to feel the feelings of grief as they come, knowing that this is just a phase that you will get through.

Get Involved in Support Groups

Join a support group. Check with your local church or hospital for grief-support groups in your area that pertain to what you are going through. It helps to be with others going through similar situations, so you won't feel alone in your thoughts and experiences.

There are a great deal of nationally recognized grief support groups that can help you start this process, or you may find that you need to start something yourself if the age ranges and circumstances of others' losses aren't in line with yours. (The need is out there, but often, it takes a select few to get things going to form more specific groups to address what more general ones cannot.)

Daily Activities

Establish a healthy daily routine of eating regularly, exercising, going to work, getting plenty of rest, and doing whatever you need each day. We will share a bit more about this in Chapter 13 but mention here that daily activities are essential in grief and life overall.

Physical Exam

Since our bodies can respond to grief in many ways, a physical examination is recommended within a couple of months after experiencing a significant loss. Each of us grieves differently, and the human body has a myriad of ways of reacting to stress and extreme sadness for extended periods. Many of these things can be directly connected to grief, from cardiovascular health to changes in weight to things like hair loss and skin changes. A doctor can help you address them (or create a plan of routine visits to monitor anything of concern).

Prepare Ahead of Special Dates and Holidays

The first year after a loss is typically the most painful. Think ahead about special dates that may be difficult as you navigate the first year. Birthdays, due dates, anniversaries, Mother's Day, Father's Day, Christmas, and Thanksgiving can all be challenging. It's the "firsts" that can be truly hard to get through—whether it's a would-be first holiday (for a baby who has never experienced the holiday before) or the first one you're celebrating without your loved one (the first of many Christmases you've had together). They are tough.

Getting through difficult days or holidays can become more manageable with a plan. Think about what you are going to do that day. Do you want to stay at home? Plan a special outing? Be with certain people? Be by yourself? Do something special to honor the loss?

We have learned over the years (from our own experiences and talking with others) that sometimes, the apprehension in waiting for a significant day can rouse more anxiety than the day itself. So, if you can think ahead and plan for the day, the actual day usually won't turn out as bad as expected. You will get through it, and with a plan, each year will get easier. This is not to say that all will be "easy." My emotions still surprise me sometimes. For whatever reason, specific days and certain years can trigger more emotions than others; that is just how grief is. The feelings of grief we continue to struggle with result from the everlasting love we hold for those we have lost over the years. **We grieve deeply because we love deeply.**

Avoid Comparing Grief

Resist comparing your grief to that of others, even the grief of someone who may be mourning a similar loss. It is human nature to form connections with other people through shared experiences, but just as you need to talk about your loss and have others listen, it is best not to speak about your loss when another person shares their story. Try to give them the space to share openly and listen. And when it's your turn, you can talk about your loss and how it's affected you. Everyone's grief experience is unique.

Reach Out

Use your experience to help others who are experiencing a similar loss. You understand better than anyone what they are experiencing, and you can be a friend who understands and inspires them to get through this. This is often just as healing for the person who reached out as it is for the person in need, providing comfort that your loss somehow helped someone else. Your loss has a purpose and was not for nothing.

Faith

In difficult times, we often look to God or a higher power to help make sense of what we are going through. Faith can help provide the strength to get us through our struggles. Renewing our faith by having regular quiet times with God (attending church, praying, reading the Bible, and reflecting on our spirituality) can help us move toward peace, acceptance of loss, and hope for the future.

Our most difficult times can help us learn important lessons and grow the most—tough times help us understand more about ourselves. Priorities and perspectives may change, our character and faith may develop and deepen, and we become more empathetic and compassionate toward those around us. We often become more compassionate, we grow stronger, and we become better people for having gone through life's challenging experiences.

Try to become aware of new strengths and increased hope you gain as time goes by. Initially, this may be difficult, but if you can make a practice of looking at the bigger picture and finding something good within the bad in a situation, it will be worth it. You will be able to hang on to the positive things that help you see things from a different perspective. Over time, this will help get you to a healthier, more peaceful place of acceptance and hope.

As you think about these things, reflect on this verse.

Not only so, but we also glory in our sufferings, because we know that suffering produces perseverance; perseverance, character; and character, hope. And hope does not put us to shame, because God's love has been poured out into our hearts through the Holy Spirit, who has been given to us.

Romans 5:3–5 (NIV)

This verse continually provides me with hope when I go through difficult times. In some of those times of suffering, I admit that I have told God I really didn't think I needed any more character-building exercises, but in and through each "trial" or "period of suffering," I learn and grow, and He teaches me more. I understand more about myself, God, people, faith, love, hope, strength, and forgiveness in each challenging experience I endure. I know there will always be more for me to learn, and there is always hope for new beginnings as a result of the past, as the next chapter discusses.

8:28

H

HOPE IN T**H**E DARKNESS

CHAPTER 8

HOPE FOR THE FUTURE

The Need for Hope

When we go through difficult times, things can seem hopeless. We all need hope to move forward, yet hope is hard to find sometimes. If you take care of yourself diligently and work through your grief and loss, a time will come when hope emerges and things begin to look brighter. You will become more comfortable in your situation and hope for the future will reappear.

Songs can bring comfort in difficult times. Melodies and lyrics can speak to us in a way that other types of stimulation and communication cannot. I have found much comfort in music throughout my life. Many songs have provided solace, especially through my losses. In the song *Hope is What We Crave* sung by the group For King and Country[15], I love how one of the verses shares how we stand and wait hoping for a drop of grace to carry us through, how we crave for the hope that is written on our soul. The words are so true. We all need hope, we have to have it to move forward.

Another song, *With Hope* by Steven Curtis Chapman[16], spoke to me while recovering and reflecting upon my losses. Again, hope is the essence of what lets us move forward day by day. In his song he shares how we can believe that everything God promised us it true so we can wait with hope, ache with hope, hold on with hope and let go with hope and move forward with hope.

Everyone needs hope because there is no incentive to move forward without it. We must come to a place of acceptance of our circumstances and hang on to hope for the future. As one season of life ends, a new season begins. No one escapes life without difficult times. When we have been mired in a difficult season, there will eventually come a time when we want to make some changes and move forward—when we are tired of our current state of mind and need hope for the future. God has instilled a drive to survive from birth and promises us hope and a future. The Bible provides us assurances of this:

"For I know the plans I have for you," declares the Lord, "plans to prosper you and not to harm you, plans to give you hope and a future."
Jeremiah 29:11 (NIV)

God promises us hope and a future. We are not guaranteed a long life free of difficulties here on Earth, but as a believer in Christ, we are guaranteed hope and a future with Him. This provides me hope while here on Earth and hope for eternity. Life on earth can be difficult, but with Him, we are assured that He is always with us to help us in times of trouble.

God is our refuge and strength, a tested help in times of trouble.
Psalm 46:1 (TLB)

A woman at our church shared an example of this one Sunday. She shared a story about being away on a business trip; she'd had a horrible day of travel trying to get back home for a family member's birthday party. She knew she would miss the party when her connecting flight was canceled. She was coming down with the flu, her bags were lost, and her wallet was stolen—it was a horrible travel day for her!

She finally got on a flight hours later than her original flight. Her seat was in the middle row of the economy section. A woman with a crying infant sat next to her. And to make matters worse, she was seated in the last row, so the seat didn't recline. It couldn't have been more uncomfortable. Then, out of the blue, the flight attendant approached her and asked her to follow her. She followed the flight attendant up to the front of the plane, where she was asked if she wanted to sit in first class. She promptly said, "Really? Of course, I would love to. What's the catch?" The flight attendant said, "There isn't a catch; just consider it a gift."

As she was sitting in her first-class reclining seat, enjoying legroom with a soft blanket on her lap and complimentary drinks and snacks in hand, she began to relax and unwind. She thought, *What a lovely place first class is.* And her flight back home was extremely comfortable. It wasn't that all her troubles were gone, but rather that her experience in first class provided a much more pleasant ride than she would have had in her cramped economy seat next to a screaming child. That is kind of how it is with God. He doesn't promise us a life without difficulties and trials, but life becomes a much lovelier ride with Him to help guide, protect, and comfort us. The difficulties we experience provide an opportunity for new perspectives, new beginnings, and a new relationship with God.

The best way to know that God is always with us is to remind ourselves of what God's Word promises us. Here are additional scriptures that assure us that God is always with us, thus offering us an endless supply of hope:

Have I not commanded you? "Be strong and courageous. Do not be frightened, and do not be dismayed, for the Lord your God is with you wherever you go."
Joshua 1:9 (NIV)

God Blesses those who mourn, for they will be comforted.
Matthew 5:4 (NLT)

Don't be afraid, for I am with you. Don't be discouraged, for I am your God. I will strengthen you and help you. I will hold you up with my victorious right hand.
Isaiah 41:10 (NLT)

So we do not look at what we can see right now, the troubles all around us, but we look forward to the joys in heaven which we have not yet seen.

The troubles will soon be over, but the joys to come will last forever.
2 Corinthians 4:18 (TLB)

"...So after you have suffered a little while, he will restore, support, and
strengthen you, and he will place you on a firm foundation."
1 Peter 5:10 (NLT)

"Do not be afraid for I have called you by name; you are mine. When
you go through deep waters, I will be with you. When you go through
rivers of difficulty, you won't drown. When you walk through fire of
oppression, you will not be burned up; the flames will not consume you.
For I am the Lord God, the Holy One of Israel, your Savior."
Isaiah 43:1–3 (TLB)

For I can do everything through Christ who gives me strength.
Philippians 4:13 (NLT)

Be strong! Be courageous! Do not be afraid of them!
For the Lord, your God will be with you.
He will neither fail you nor forsake you.
Deuteronomy 31:6 (TLB)

These are all beautiful verses that provide the assurance of God's continued love, help, and everlasting presence in our lives. If we are open, we will receive the hope we need to carry us through whatever challenges we face.

The serenity prayer[17] has become a standard in Alcoholics Anonymous (AA) and mental wellness communities, and with good reason. It opens as follows:

"God, grant me the serenity to accept the things I cannot change, courage to change the things I can, and wisdom to know the difference."

When it seems that hope is lost, you will come to the decision point of asking yourself a critical question: ***Do I want to move forward with hope or stay where I am?***

Sometimes, you must get to a place of hopelessness to realize that you want to make some changes. Nothing will change until you are ready to take action and make changes. You must take steps to push yourself toward healing and hope. This looks different for everyone. Some steps might be to join a support group, check into rehab, mend a broken relationship, ask for or provide forgiveness for the pain caused to others, or ask God for forgiveness.

If you are angry with God or don't have a relationship with Him, ask God to relieve your anger and show you who He is and how much He loves you. Ask Him to bring people into your life to comfort, guide, and support you, or ask God to help your unbelief. Take steps to accept your situation and realize that you can't change the past. All you can do is hang on to hope and make wise choices for the future. Take steps toward finding hope, and eventually, you will see new beginnings emerge.

I have learned that if we move toward acceptance of our circumstances and rest in hope for the future with faith, we can handle the challenges we encounter in a healthier way and ultimately live a fulfilled, purposeful, and abundant life.

As we move forward with acceptance, faith, hope for the future, and new beginnings, it doesn't mean we won't experience setbacks along the way, as the next chapter, "Emotional Roller Coaster," discusses.

8:28

E

HOPE IN THE DARKNESS

CHAPTER 9

EMOTIONAL ROLLER COASTER

Setbacks – Just When You Thought Things Were Getting Better

The summer before my brother, Terry, died, my dad collapsed and was found incoherent on the floor of his study. His neighbor called 9-1-1, and he was rushed to the hospital. I was notified immediately, so I packed a bag and headed again for Northern California. When I spoke with the doctor, I was informed that my dad had a condition related to sleep apnea that caused a buildup of carbon dioxide and dangerously low oxygen levels. This condition, we learned, could be fatal, and it caused him to become delusional. He became paranoid and lost all sense of reality. The only way to bring his levels to a safe place was to have him wear a breathing mask or what is known as Continuous Positive Airway Pressure (CPAP) therapy, but every time they tried to put it on, he fought the nurses and doctors because he believed in his mind that the people in the hospital were trying to kill him. I was the only one who could calm him down, so we talked for the entire six hours while I drove up north to the hospital. I had to reassure him that the people in the hospital were only trying to help him and that I would be there soon. I stayed with him in the hospital day and night for a week until they were able to balance out his levels. His short-term memory and sense of reality were utterly gone. He didn't know what year it was or where he was.

My dad was brilliant. He received his Ph.D. in Psychology from Stanford University and loved learning and research, so, naturally, it would have been very disturbing for him to know he had lost his mind. In this state, he believed he was the School Superintendent for the Oakland School District (where he had worked for over twenty years) and in a hospital near where he had lived thirty-five years prior. He had lost thirty-five years of his most recent memory. My dad had no idea that his daughter and wife had died, and we didn't have the heart to tell him because we weren't sure how he would react.

At one point, one of the doctors told me to give up on him ever getting his mind back and to simply let him go. She said he wouldn't get any better and that all treatments should stop. We had a family meeting with the doctor, and our daughter spoke up and said that giving up on him wasn't an option. So, we all agreed that we would do whatever it took to bring Grandpa back to reality.

I sat with him for days, and we talked about many things, most of which made no sense. He told me stories about things I knew were not true, but they were real and true in his mind. He was in and out of consciousness and was often agitated. To calm him, I often played hymns on my iPad. My dad loved hymns. He had grown up with them. His father had been a pastor, and his mother had played piano and organ at their church. When I played the music, there were sweet times when my dad would hum or softly sing the words to the hymns with his eyes closed. One of his favorites was "How Great Thou Art," which will forever bring me to tears.

Hearing my dad sing hymns in the hospital bed was a treasured gift and something I will never forget. I remember once, in the middle of the night, after days of no change, I prayed at his bedside for God to either completely heal and restore his mind or to just take him to heaven. A social worker came into his hospital room the following day and started talking to him. I had brought a family photo album to try and help restore his memory, so she asked him questions about the people in the pictures. She asked him questions about his life story, and as she asked more questions, he began to share more and more until he shared everything up to the present time. He remembered everything, even losing my mom and sister, which made him extremely sad, of course, but we had my dad back!

It truly was a miracle. God answered my prayer in completely restoring his mind to what it was before entering the hospital. He was able to come home, and we were able to enjoy him in our lives for another year. Such a tremendous gift! Our family and friends were able to have additional visits with him. He celebrated his eightieth birthday with his most cherished friends and family and gave a beautiful tribute at Terry's memorial service.

I am so thankful for that additional year! His mind was strong until the end when his body could no longer fight, and we got to experience that precious time with him for a bit longer. When his life was ending, and we knew that time was short, I found myself giving assurances and permission to let go as I'd done with our other precious family members. Though I was the last one remaining in our immediate family, I told him I would be okay. I reminded him that he would be with Mom, Darlene, Terry, and so many others whom he loved and had lost over the years. I assured him my kids, Rick, wonderful friends, and faith would help me through it all. I remember having that conversation with him early one morning, and by the time I went to the kitchen to get a cup of coffee and return to his bedside, his heart had stopped. I don't think he wanted me to watch him take his last breath. He went peacefully on his terms, and I'm so grateful for that. Yet, once again, I was on the emotional roller coaster of grief.

Just when you start to get back into a regular routine and begin to accept your loss, you may be hit with a wave of emotions that feel like the loss has just happened, or you may be facing another loss. Often, between seven and ten months after people experience a significant loss, they tell us they have had a setback and feel as if it just happened, like they are experiencing those early grief feelings and emotions all over again. We don't know exactly why this happens, but we believe it is simply because life goes on around us even though we are still grieving. When the initial loss occurs, family members and friends surround you with love, care, and attention, but after a few months pass, everyone tends to move on with their lives. Busyness and everyday routines resume, and the sympathy cards, meals, calls, and notes start to dwindle. People don't want to bring up the loss again for fear of upsetting you, but what they don't understand is that you are still thinking about your loss constantly. Everyone else's lives seem happy and continue in the same trajectory. Those who are still grieving continue to struggle and find it hard to see or feel joy amid all the emotions of loss.

When these emotional surprises come up, it is good to have a plan. How will you handle the situation when some trigger hurls you down that big dip of the rollercoaster? It is difficult to predict what those triggers might be, but if you can think about what the worst-case scenario might be and how you might handle it, you may find some help and comfort in having that situation worked out in your head before it (or something similar) happens.

Two months after we lost Matthew, a family member plopped his newborn son down in Rick's arms, thinking it would be helpful for Rick to hold another baby, but Rick was entirely unprepared to hold another baby so soon. It was as if someone had placed a bomb in his arms. Shaking and completely blindsided, Rick didn't know what to do in the situation, so he immediately passed the baby back to his father and quickly left the room to recover. We could have never expected the situation, but if we had considered some of the most uncomfortable situations, we might have been more prepared to handle the situation differently. I know that experience stuck with Rick for a very long time. Rick desperately wanted to hold Matthew again, and the choice to hold another baby should have been on Rick's terms, not because someone else forced him to. I'm not saying that we should continually obsess over situations that may happen, but it can be helpful to have a couple of options and ways out of difficult situations, so you aren't caught completely off guard.

On that note, having a sign or signal between couples or friends in public can be helpful to alert each other if they need to be rescued from a conversation or leave the situation. No matter where or when, if one or the other gives the signal, it means they need to leave. It could be because they are in an uncomfortable conversation, or maybe they saw or heard something triggering and need a quick escape before completely melting down (the plummeting feeling on the roller coaster).

One question I often heard and eventually had to confront was, "How many children do you have?" Over the years, I have learned that I answer that question differently depending on who is asking. With some people, I might say, I have two on earth and two in heaven. To others, I may say I have two—Ryan and Avery. It is an internal conflict because if I say two, acknowledging Ryan and Avery (my living children), I feel like I'm dishonoring Matthew and our other baby in heaven. If I say I have two in heaven and two on earth, it may make the person asking the question feel bad for asking in the first place, or it may prompt additional questions for a sometimes lengthy conversation that I may or may not be up for.

Many people have said (to me and others in deep grief), "God will never give you more than you can handle." For some reason, they think this is a positive thing to say when people have gone through difficulties. When they said this to me, I understood it as, "You must be very strong. God sure has given you a lot to handle." It conveys that God thought so highly of me and planned to heap losses on me with the knowledge that I was strong and could handle it. But after I heard people tell me this, I was not comforted; instead, I felt upset with them for thinking that of me, much less of God.

This sentiment stems from an often-misquoted Bible verse. The verse actually pertains to temptation, stating that God will never allow us to be tempted more than we can handle, and He will always provide us with a way out. I've included this verse here for a couple of reasons. First, I hope people will understand the context of the verse and not apply it inappropriately to difficulties, suffering, and certain trials of life. Second, I want to show how God can help us when we might be blindsided and tempted to respond with unforgiveness, unhealthy anger, or resentment. If we look to Him for guidance, God can and will provide us with ways out of situations.

The temptations in your life are no different from what others experience. And God is faithful. He will not allow the temptation to be more than you can stand. When you are tempted, he will show you a way out so that you can endure.
1 Corinthians 10:13 (NLT)

Sometimes, we can "derail" the roller coaster by communicating and educating people to help them avoid saying or doing things that may cause us to remain on this ride longer than we should. We can share our needs and what to say and what not to say, as Chapter 3 discusses. Certain people may continually trigger you and keep you riding the twists and turns of the roller coaster. If so, you may need to distance yourself from those people and set boundaries until you are stronger and can better handle what they say. (And there may be times when a relationship is lost because things may never change.)

There are many ups and downs on the grief journey. Be patient with yourself and realize that you are not losing your mind. If you find yourself in that intense seven-to-ten-month period after a loss, just know that this phase will not last as long as the time of the initial loss, especially if you can understand that this is normal. You are still grieving, so you will inevitably continue to have good days and bad days.

Grief is a day-to-day, moment-by-moment journey. Returning to some of the original information we started with may be helpful if you have a setback. Review the "Grief Survival Guidelines" (see Chapter 7), and make sure you take care of yourself in those ways. Review some of your journal writings to assess where you were and how much you've progressed over the weeks and months. Continue learning about what you are going through and lean into your emotions. There are plenty of resources online to read and learn how others have survived their losses. Join a local support group (virtually through social media or in person) and connect with people who have experienced similar situations. Again, please refer to www.828HOPE.com for additional resources.

Attend church regularly and soak in the love, strength, and comfort a relationship with God and other people of faith can offer. Acknowledge that you are still grieving and give yourself the grace and permission to do so. There may be a feeling of desperation (from others or self-imposed) to be "normal" again, but you have a new normal. You are a changed person because of your loss. Peace and other "happier" emotions will be experienced in new and different ways as you live with and learn to be comfortable in your grief.

One day, you will look back and realize that you are stronger and better for having been through what you went through. This is not to say that all your questions will be answered or that your grief and memories of the loss will be gone. There may always be triggers, but eventually, you will be through the worst of the twists and turns of the emotional roller coaster and on a gentler ride.

Chapter 10 examines how the roller coaster of emotions and desperation for peace and understanding can lead to daily deliverance and hope for the future.

8:28

D

HOPE IN THE DARKNESS

DESPERATION AND DAILY DELIVERANCE

Desperate to Be Delivered from Grief!

I was devastated after losing my dad—my last immediate family member. Although I had my close family unit with Rick and our kids, no one could understand what I was feeling. My family and friends were exceptionally compassionate and offered much help and support, but it was so hard to describe what I was going through. It was the oddest reality to have lost everyone in my family—everyone I had grown up knowing. I felt as if I were an orphan. No parents and no siblings. How could anyone possibly understand the depth of my grief and what I was feeling?

I arranged a graveside burial service, memorial service, and a "celebration of life" gathering for extended family and friends. These beautiful celebrations honored not only my dad but also the rest of my immediate family, who had died before him. I longed to rehearse with my dad what I would say at his service—just as I had done with him before for services held for my sister, mother, and brother. Since he was now gone, too, I was on my own for this one. Despite the caring support and love from dear friends, Rick, and our kids, I couldn't imagine how I would make it through speaking at yet another memorial service. Oh, how I missed all of them!

After the memorial service, I stayed at my parents' house for a few weeks to sort through everything. As executor of the trust, I had much paperwork and personal items to go through. I decided I wasn't ready to sell the house but knew I would need to clear everything out to get it ready to rent or sell at some point. I donated many items and sold things that didn't have sentimental value.

Although many people offered to help, I felt I was the only one who could go through everything. Only I knew the stories behind what was essential to keep and what was okay to let go of. It was a lot of work, but it kept me busy and allowed me time to grieve. I went through pictures and memories of my life while growing up and cried buckets of tears. Emotional as it was, I found it healing to have that time to grieve in my way and in my own time.

On the last night before heading back to my home in Southern California, I got to a point where I felt incapacitated and incapable of making any more decisions. The house was virtually empty except for a few boxes in the corner of one of the rooms. A dear friend who lived around the corner came over to bring me some food since I had not been eating regularly over the weeks of clearing everything out of my parents' home. When she entered the house, I was standing and staring at the boxes with a dazed look. After weeks of sorting through a lifetime of memories, I was left with a few boxes in the corner. I was emotionally and physically exhausted and couldn't decide what to do with the remaining boxes. When my friend asked me what I needed help with, I couldn't answer her. I felt paralyzed, and then I just broke down and sobbed. Thankfully, my friend helped me move the remaining boxes out of the house so I could drive home to be with my husband and kids and refocus.

Gratitude Journals

I was desperate to feel "normal" again! Desperate to have my life back! Desperate for peace and hope in knowing I would be okay. After losing six beloved family members over six years, I was desperate to find ways to cope and work through my grief. I had heard about "gratitude journals" being helpful in times of need, so I decided to give it a try. Many people use a gratitude journal to help hang on to the positive things even amid difficult times, while others use prayer journals to record their thoughts and prayers, including those that God has already answered.

I have learned that we can benefit from writing down our thoughts and prayers and that recording things we are thankful for can be especially helpful. While previous chapters have encouraged journaling, a gratitude journal is somewhat different but similarly beneficial. A growing number of studies show the benefits of gratitude journaling, all of which suggest that gratitude journaling may improve sleep quality and well-being.[18] These studies have shown a link between giving thanks and sleeping habits. According to a study from the University of Minnesota, participants were asked to list positive events at the end of each day and include why they made them happy. This simple exercise lowered the participants' stress levels, and they reported feeling calmer at night.[19]

EXERCISE 6:

Keep a gratitude journal by your bed or start a list on your phone to jot down what you are thankful for each day.

Review the list each night before you go to sleep or each morning when you wake up and start a new day. Some days, you may only have one or two things you can think of to be thankful for, and you may have more on other days. Don't worry about the number of items on your list. Thinking about what you are thankful for can be your daily deliverance from grief.

Your daily entries don't need to be deep or take much time. It can be as simple as this:

- I'm thankful for my family.
- I'm thankful for the book I'm reading.
- I'm thankful I can read.
- I'm thankful for breakfast.
- I'm thankful for the sunshine on my face.
- I'm thankful for the call from my mom.

You can elaborate on each item, explaining why you are thankful for each day or keeping it simple. If you are elaborating on each item, be sure not to let any negativity seep in. This exercise is about being thankful and bringing in good feelings and emotions. No exceptions.

Prayer Journals

Keeping a prayer journal is another good practice to add to your daily deliverance. My sister, Darlene, had many examples of how God works in and through others to help us through our darkest times, especially through prayer. Similar to Exercise 6, Darlene kept a prayer journal, writing down her thoughts and prayers—and her answered prayers, too.

Throughout her battle with cancer and until she could fight no longer, her eyes were opened to how God used people, perfectly timed gifts, and prayers to help her and help others. The following is a letter of thanks she sent out shortly before she died, sharing how God continually provided her with extraordinary gifts and explaining the effectiveness of prayer.

Dear Ones,

A year ago, I broke my arm, so I've been reflecting especially about just how much people have given me this year. I've not wanted to share the ups and downs of the oncological roller coaster, but there has been so much prayer surrounding my life that I want you to know how I think God has answered.

I believe that God uses people to reach out to us on earth. He uses good doctors, medicine, and therapists, but also friends, families, and husbands to wrap His arms around us. There are so many times when I felt God's closeness—in the hospital, for example—that I've lost count. Thank you from the bottom of my heart for all the acts of kindness you have shown me—meals, cards, notes, calls, and especially prayer, despite your busyness. He hears your prayers and answers them in ways we never could imagine.

Here are just a few ways I think he has used you to help me. Imagine what He has done for the others you have prayed for and those who have prayed for you!

- *Some of you have prayed for encouragement: From the first pre-op meeting eight years ago, through nearly every medical encounter, every ER visit, every visit to the hospital, every transfusion, He has placed a believer near me who often whispered under his or her breath, "I'm praying for you."*

- *Others have prayed for healing: In July, the skin invasion, which no one gave any hope of actually healing, did, in fact, heal almost completely. The cancer itself has been held at bay another year so far, even though the original prognosis offered a much grimmer timeline. No wonder the doctors are amazed!*

- *When you prayed for comfort and joy this year, I got to enjoy a spring and summer of visits (some planned and some not) from family and friends, and just being with my husband and kids.*

- *When you prayed that the infection would be taken from my port, He took away the port itself! This gave way to a summer unencumbered by IVs and similar paraphernalia.*

- *When you prayed for diminished pain, I got well enough to take our daughter to college in Massachusetts and then later to make the trip there again for Parents' Weekend.*

- *When you prayed for strength, I got to take ever-increasing little walks in my neighborhood, and even at the local Trader Joe's! In fact, even though my physical therapist thought walking with a cane was the best I could expect, I've been cane-free for about a month now!*

- *Prayers for nourishment brought meals for my family, days, and even weeks without nausea, and a return to a more natural way of eating.*

- *Prayers for spiritual strength gave way to unexpected but much-needed devotionals, or to a conversation, a kind word spoken, or an unplanned visit, and always at just the right time. I even received a bulletin board full of scriptural passages to remind me, and others, of who God is.*

- *Some people's prayers for lifting my spirits produced deliveries of the most beautiful flowers and plants I've ever seen, which uplifted me, but also all who saw them. Or a gift of music or poetry, and on just the right day. All these have reminded me of who God is, but they have also touched those who have heard them, seen them, or enjoyed them along with me.*

- *A basket full of prayerful cards and letters has inspired me day by day as I received your mail, but it has also been a reminder to those who have seen all this that they make a difference—and such a difference—"simply" by sending a card to someone else. For example, I ended up lending one gift—a little book on prayer—to another praying friend, who showed it to another praying friend, who then purchased multiple copies for her praying friends! The list of blessings goes on and on.*

So, if you're wondering whether prayer matters, it does. And sometimes, you're the answer to someone else's prayer, whether you know it or not. What I know without a doubt is how grateful I am to God, and you, as Thanksgiving approaches.

Love, Darlene

Darlene's letter is a beautiful example of how God works through us and in the lives of others as a result of prayer. Even though we may never understand how and why God answers prayers as He does, we know that all prayers are answered in some way. Our prayers may not be answered as we would like, but we must trust that God is good and has a plan and purpose for all things. I love how she shares the notion that we don't fully understand how prayer works, but it does work. And sometimes, though we may not realize it, *we* are an answer to someone else's prayer.

One of Darlene's favorite verses was this:

Do not be anxious about anything, but in everything by prayer and supplication with thanksgiving let your requests be made known to God. And the peace of God, which surpasses all understanding, will guard your hearts and your minds in Christ Jesus.
Philippians 4:6–7 (ESV).

There are many benefits a gratitude or prayer journal can provide, including but not limited to the following:

✧ Lowering stress levels.

✧ Providing a sense of calmness at night.

✧ Providing a new perspective on what is important to you and what you genuinely appreciate in your life.

✧ Gaining clarity on what you want to have more of in your life and what you can cut from your life.

✧ Helping you focus on what truly matters.

✧ Learning more about yourself and becoming more self-aware of what you want for the future.

✧ Providing a safe place—a place for your eyes only so that you can write anything you feel without judgment.

✧ Offering a place to review and adjust your attitude by reflecting and seeing the positive things in your life.

✧ Beginning a relationship with God.

✧ Strengthening your trust and faith in God to see how He hears and answers prayers.

As you begin to change your mindset from dwelling on your loss to one of gratitude for the good things in your life, you will start looking for things to be grateful for. When you are having a difficult day and possibly again asking, *Why me?* look in your gratitude journal or prayer journal to see and appreciate the good things in your life. By opening our thoughts and minds to see the beauty and gifts around us and focusing on the things we can be grateful for, we will gain a new perspective on life and perhaps see many answered prayers. We will begin to see and understand the bigger picture and trust God's plan.

8:28

A

HOPE IN THE DARKNESS

CHAPTER 11

ASKING AGAIN – WHY ME?

What Have I Learned? Why *Not* Me?

We are who we are as a result of the things that happen in our lives. As much as I may wish that certain things had not happened or had somehow happened differently, the totality of everything good and bad has made me who I am today, and I'm thankful for that. The most difficult things I have experienced have made me stronger, more compassionate, and more appreciative of my relationships, as well as my time here on earth. I could ask over and over again, *Why me?* but instead, I have made a conscious effort to ask, *Why **not** me?* I wouldn't wish the losses I have been through on anyone else. These things happened to me for whatever reason, and it is up to me to decide what to do with them.

We always have a choice in how we will handle the things with which we are faced. As my mother-in-law used to say, "You can make things better, or you can make things worse." Our choices can't always change a situation's outcome, but we have a choice in how we will handle the outcome. Choices, whether good or bad, have consequences, and we have a choice about how to handle those consequences.

A person can certainly say, "Could anything be worse than what I am going through?" Many situations seem horrible, and you may think nothing could be worse. It's a profoundly personal assessment, given a particular set of circumstances and feelings the situation may elicit.

But if you honestly considered the situation, you could probably imagine something even worse—which, weirdly, somehow helps.

This can take time to understand, which is one reason support groups can be so helpful. Hearing other people's stories helps you realize that you are not alone, and that other people are also going through difficult situations. And yes, as much as it's advised to avoid comparison, human nature means that you sometimes look at others and think, "Well, I sure wouldn't want to be going through what they are going through." So, instead of asking, "Why me?" ask, "Why **not** me?" Try to look at how you are growing and becoming stronger as you go through whatever you are struggling with.

You will get through it. It takes time, but you will see how you have grown, changed, and become stronger as a result. We don't want the difficult situations in our lives to negatively define who we are or who we become. To achieve this, try to change your mindset so that the experiences in your life represent new perspectives and positive qualities.

Sometimes, people have to wrestle with the nature of God, and it becomes a personal battle in which they seek to determine whether the notion that "God is good" is accurate in all situations. As discussed in Chapter 5, many people are angry with God, which is okay. He can handle it. But what matters is what you do with that anger.

Do you want to hang on to it, or do you want to release it and come to a belief that God is good? For some, hanging on to their anger promotes a victim mentality. When you experience anger, it is nearly impossible not to feel like a victim in your circumstances. You feel powerless, unjustifiably wronged, betrayed, judged, taken advantage of, or mistreated. There is an innocence associated with being a victim. Since anger is typically volatile, it can provide a sense of control, righteousness, and pride in defending what is being attacked, so there can be a desire to stay angry. For me, I needed and wanted God *with* me rather than against me. I know He loves me and has a plan for my life. I made a decision early on to choose to run to God when times are tough rather than run away from Him. I knew I couldn't endure difficult times without His love, comfort, peace, and hope. I needed to trust in His promises, so instead of being angry at God, I chose to run straight to Him to help me through it all.

With time, in and through my losses, I started to understand some of the "why" questions as they pertained to me and what I was to learn from them. It has taken time to get to this point, but I can honestly say that I have peace in knowing that all I've been through and will continue to go through in life is part of His perfect timing and plan. Though I didn't appreciate or understand it at the time, I can honestly say I am a better person for going through the things I've gone through, and they have made me who I am today.

Some of the following could be answers to why I had to go through the losses and the gain I received as a result. Through my losses, my relationship with God has grown deeper and stronger. Through the loss of Matthew and our other baby, I gained compassion and empathy for others going through the pain of loss. We have been able to help hundreds of people through similar losses, and we have made beautiful friendships along the way. Through the loss of my sister, my eyes were opened to the power of prayer and how to be an example of love and grace to others. Through the loss of my mom, I learned about faith, heaven, and the deep bond between mother and child. (I also strive to be an example of faith and love to my children and future grandchildren.) Through losing my brother, I've seen and admired the passionate love and pure strength to endure for another and how powerful and meaningful friendships are. And through the loss of my dad, I have learned the importance of marriage. My dad was lost without my mom, and he wanted me to know how important marriage is and how he wished he had told my mom more often how much he loved and appreciated her. I hope to set a similarly loving example for our children in their marriages and as they raise their families.

These are all things I wouldn't have seen or known without going through the losses I went through. I can say that some of these things answer the "why" questions. Do I wish each of them were still here? Absolutely! Each loss has been extremely painful for me, but through them, I have learned beautiful lessons on which I can build the rest of my life and live in honor of these amazing people. It took me some time to get here, but I can honestly say that God is good. I know He loves me and everyone equally, with a love far greater and more significant than we could ever imagine. I trust in Him and His plan. God has a plan, a perfect place, and a time for everything.

The concept of God's perfect plan is beautifully explained through the lyrics of the song Turn Turn Turn; To Everything There is a Season written in 1959 by Pete Seeger. This song became an international hit in 1965 when it was released by the American folk-rock group, The Byrds. What many may not realize, however, is that the lyrics are based on *Ecclesiastes 3* from the Old Testament.

A Time for Everything

For everything, there is a season,
a time for every activity under heaven.

A time to be born and a time to die.
A time to plant and a time to harvest.

A time to kill and a time to heal.
A time to tear down and a time to build up.

A time to cry and a time to laugh.
A time to grieve and a time to dance.

A time to scatter stones and a time to gather stones.
A time to embrace and a time to turn away.

A time to search and a time to quit searching.
A time to keep and a time to throw away.

A time to tear and a time to mend.
A time to be quiet and a time to speak.

A time to love and a time to hate.
A time for war and a time for peace.

Ecclesiastes 3:1-8 (NLT)

You may need to have some conversations with God to realize that He loves you and that He is good. God loves everyone equally and doesn't single out anyone. He created each one of us in His own unique and beautiful way. He is in control and has a plan and purpose for everything. We can reflect God's goodness in our lives and those around us when we accept that God is good and ultimately wants the best for us.

Why did we go through what we went through if not to help others going through similar experiences? Why *not* me? There is always a choice as to how we will handle a situation. We can hang on to our hurts and become bitter and resentful or we can choose to use our experiences to help ourselves heal by helping others. Healing, comfort, and hope can come out of our darkest times, and in that, we can rejoice.

8:28

R

HOPE IN THE DARKNESS

CHAPTER 12

REJOICE... REALLY?

Finding the Blessings

The Bible tells us in 1 Thessalonians 5:16–18 (NIV), *"Rejoice always, pray continually, give thanks in all circumstances."*

This seems like sound Biblical advice, but seriously, how do we do that? We have to be open to see blessings. In everything, we are to give thanks, and we are to find blessings rather than burdens. This can be exceedingly difficult in situations of loss and grief.

Romans 5:3–5 (TLB) states:

We can rejoice, too, when we run into problems and trials, for we know that they are good for us—they help us learn to be patient. And patience develops strength of character in us and helps us trust God more each time we use it until finally our hope and faith are strong and steady. Then, when that happens, we are able to hold our heads high no matter what happens and know that all is well, for we know how dearly God loves us, and we feel this warm love everywhere within us because God has given us the Holy Spirit to fill our hearts with his love.

After receiving Darlene's letter about prayer (shared in Chapter 10), a dear friend suggested I write about how God showed up in other ways during the year before her death and in her last days. Below, I recount how I saw God show up in my life (and in the lives of others) in so many ways. Through these journal entries (from my last visit with my sister), I was able to reflect on the time I spent with her that year and how I saw God in all of it. He always works out the details so beautifully, even during the most difficult times, and in that, we can rejoice!

While in the hospital last spring, God made Himself visible every day with gifts of hope and faith. Darlene was blessed with many "God moments." Her roommate during one of her hospital stays was a Christian. One Sunday, Darlene was thinking about how much she wished she could be at her church when in walked her roommate's pastor and choir. The pastor prayed and read scripture, and the choir sang. What a gift it was for Darlene to share in this experience! Even when Darlene couldn't attend church, He brought the church to her.

One day while in the hospital, Darlene's Bible study group brought her a memo board filled with Bible verses and affirmations. The board was placed prominently in her hospital room for all to see. As hospital staff, friends, and family visited her room, everyone would ask about the beautiful memo board. This gave her the perfect opportunity to share what her special Bible study group had done for her. It opened many doors to witness and share her faith with others.

During another hospital visit, Darlene was feeling apprehensive about a blood transfusion she was going to have; she wished she could have someone with her to give her a little extra encouragement before the procedure. All of a sudden, a nurse walked into her room to make sure she was ready for the transfusion. Surprisingly, the nurse turned out to be a family friend and a strong Christian. This nurse prayed with Darlene and helped give her peace and comfort throughout the procedure. Darlene knew the assignment of this special nurse was a gift from God.

While in the hospital, Darlene felt God's presence constantly. She was given gifts daily from doctors, nurses, friends, and family. She was ministered to and was able to minister to others. As much as God gave her strength through the people He brought into her hospital room to care for her, He also provided opportunities for Darlene to share her faith with others. Many roommates shared how much she helped them during their hospital visit. She read scripture, prayed, and offered support to all her roommates. They all expressed how they were lifted by her love and strong faith. She was able to witness to others continually during her hospital visits.

Another blessing was the "Care Page" blog that Barry, her husband, had set up. It allowed him to update and keep in touch with everyone about Darlene's situation. It also allowed others to share thoughts and messages of encouragement, faith, and, love with Darlene and her family. This "blog" was absolutely amazing. There were so many wonderful blessings that came out of this. Many were exposed to Darlene's faith through her battle with cancer, and it also provided an avenue for others to express their faith and prayers. All who read the messages were exposed to the love and peace we have in Jesus Christ. It became an amazing tool for witnessing to others.

Even after coming home from the hospital, Darlene continued to feel His presence daily. One day, she was wishing she had a good basic daily devotional she could read, since her other Bible study had finished up and she couldn't attend Bible studies outside the home anymore. Lo and behold, without her ever mentioning her desire for a simple daily devotional that she could manage, her Bible study group came by with a gift for her: a daily devotional. She again felt God's presence; He continually strengthened her in the knowledge that He provides us all we need even before we can say what it is we want. He knows our hearts and deepest desires, and He continually provides for our needs.

Darlene ended up in the hospital again. Her last lucid conversation had been with Amy, her daughter, a few days before. Shortly after the conversation with Amy, she had returned a call to me, since I had tried calling her while she was on the phone. Darlene was barely able to speak, but she seemed to have something important to share. It was very hard to make sense of her thoughts and words, but in discussing things with Barry, who was listening on the other end, we believe she was trying to tell me that we had all already said everything we needed to say to one another, so there was no need for everyone to come out to see her in her last days. She had said that she didn't want people to feel the way she had felt when she was forced to visit and say goodbye to our dying Grandpa when she was a young girl. She shared that she and Barry had talked to Amy and Mark (their son) about the timing of Darlene's death and asked for prayer about how things would happen. That conversation with me was her last. I believe her prayer was answered. As I see it, the timing worked out perfectly in so many ways.

A good friend, Roger, graciously offered me a ticket to come and visit Darlene. The scheduling worked out perfectly with flights and Rick's work schedule so that I could make the trip.

Amy's timing worked out perfectly for an arrival time from Philly shortly after my flight landed from California so that we didn't need to make multiple trips to and from the airport. This provided time for me and Amy to share some good talks and cries before Mom and Dad and even Mark arrived.

Mom and Dad's timing worked out perfectly for them to come and visit after mom's cancer treatment in L.A. They were able to fly in and out of Los Angeles, ensuring she could meet her next scheduled appointment.

Wednesday was a difficult yet beautiful day. Dad wrote a beautiful 11-page letter, reminiscing about Darlene's life. He included stories from the night she was conceived through kindergarten, proms, Stanford, her time of study in France, her falling in love, the wedding, UCLA, New York, Mark and Amy, and living in Pennsylvania. The letter, which Dad had sent with the hope that Darlene would read it herself, set the stage and provided a beautiful backdrop for us all to reminisce and share stories about Darlene's life. Barry read the letter amidst tears shed by all who listened, and, again, God's timing was perfect. I believe Darlene heard every story and enjoyed every moment of Dad's heartfelt letter along with all of us. It also allowed Barry to reflect and share some things that I think would have otherwise been left unsaid.

Beautiful gifts of prayer were provided throughout the day from friends who stopped by to visit Darlene and the family. Beautiful prayers of comfort, hope, and peace were given as we gathered at her bedside and laid hands on Darlene.

The hospital staff who had come to know and love Darlene came by to check in on her and Barry even when they weren't on duty. Two glorious hymns, "Great is Thy Faithfulness" and "The Sparrow," were sung by one of the nurses, which brought tears to all our eyes. Our crying during the songs caused the nurse to cry as well, but she was able to complete the last song. It was an incredible gift by a beautiful nurse, and again the timing was perfect because we were all present to share in such a special gift of music and worship. The nurse had sung "How Great Thou Art" on Friday, and Darlene had asked her if she also knew "Great is Thy Faithfulness." The nurse didn't know all the words, so she took the time to learn the song and various verses so that she could sing for us all on Wednesday. I'm sure Darlene could hear the music. It was like listening to a piece of heaven. And again, the timing was perfect..

Mark made it in time to visit his mom. He arrived about 10 p.m. that Wednesday evening. I believe Darlene was hanging on and waiting for her eldest to arrive. I thought that she might then permit herself to be with God. She fought an incredible battle, but it was time: She had done her job and all she could do here on earth.

Darlene made it through the night and was stable throughout the day. Mom, Amy, and I brought some stitchery, knitting, and crocheting materials to keep us busy while we waited in Darlene's room. A couple of women she worked with brought her a beautiful and bright quilt that we laid over Darlene. It made the room so much brighter. Mom, Dad, and I stayed with her until about 11 p.m., and Mark, Amy, and Barry spent the night in her room.

Mom wasn't feeling well the next day, so Dad and I went to the hospital. Dad didn't stay long because he wanted to get back to be with Mom. When I arrived, Barry and Amy were there. Mark had returned to the house to get a couple of things, and when he got back, he brought his guitar. Also, Mark told us that an internship he had applied for had been approved, which was something Darlene had been concerned about and had hoped would be taken care of before Thanksgiving. Mark proceeded to play some beautiful music on his guitar. He played one of her favorite songs, and then he played "Misty," and Barry began to sing. It brought tears to my eyes listening to them sing and play such a beautiful song for Darlene. Mark set his guitar down and we were all sitting and talking for a few minutes. Then we heard Darlene give a little cough and gurgle. We alerted the nurses and they came in to take her pulse. Darlene let out a couple more sighs and she was gone. It was so peaceful that we weren't even sure what had happened. Her last breath was at about 2:50 p.m. Mom and Dad arrived about fifteen minutes later. We were all able to spend time with her, we kissed her beautiful face, stroked her hand, and said our goodbyes. For such a difficult situation, God made it as beautiful and peaceful as possible. I think Darlene just needed a couple more things in place for her to let go. She needed the knowledge that both Mark and Amy were settled and on the right track for the future, and she also needed to hear Mark play for her one last time. She is now with the Lord and free of pain, and *for that, I am grateful, although I will miss her dearly.*

Shortly before our last conversation, Darlene shared something with me that our mom had shared years ago. Mom had told her that no one could ever take prayer away from us. We can still pray even if we can't talk or move our bodies. Darlene had always hung on to these words, especially while in the hospital, because there were times when she was so weak that she couldn't move or speak, but she could still pray. Prayer itself is such a wonderful gift from God. It is extremely difficult to rejoice through suffering, but we can look for the blessings and find things to be thankful for. Even in the darkest times, if we are open to looking at things from a new and different perspective, we can rejoice. It may be something very big or something very small, but if you truly look, there is always something helpful or positive to be found. Along with rejoicing in what we experience, we also need to keep moving, trying, and believing we will make it through whatever we are going through, as we will see in the next chapter.

8:28

K

HOPE IN THE DARKNESS

CHAPTER 13

KEEP MOVING, KEEP TRYING, KEEP BELIEVING

Day by Day, Moment by Moment

Two years after my father passed away, when we were starting to adjust to living with our losses, Rick received a phone call from the San Diego Police Department sharing the news that Rick's older sister had been found lifeless in her home. Was another family member gone? How can that be? Devastated once more, Rick rushed to San Diego to figure out what had happened and make arrangements for yet another memorial service and celebration of life. It seemed unbelievable that our family was again experiencing another significant loss, and we had to deal with grief head-on.

When we go through loss, we need to keep moving—day by day and moment by moment. We must keep trying and believing that we will make it through our hard times. Admittedly, some days are tougher than others, and you are just wiped out. You are tired of grieving and no longer want to be in pain; it is normal to feel that way. The key is allowing yourself those times of grief and sadness, but once you acknowledge and feel those feelings, you must keep moving forward, pushing through it, and beginning to live again. Even if it's nothing more than simply getting out of bed; that is a step toward healing.

Try to do a little more each day—maybe get out of bed and then make the bed. Those are moving steps; you can add things like making your bed and then making yourself breakfast. A big step may be running an errand—something you probably didn't give a second thought to before your loss. But when you're working through grief, some of the most menial tasks (going to the store or the post office) can feel overwhelming.

At some point, you may have to force yourself to become more active. If you're not ready to go to a gym or to take a walk (or run) in your neighborhood, you can still be active inside. Find a yoga or meditation program on TV or online, or download a fitness app on your preferred device. Walk up and downstairs or around your house a few times. There are many ways you can still get some exercise without leaving your home.

When you're depressed or in heavy grief, your energy levels can drop drastically. So, even if you don't feel like it, getting up and moving is vital for your health. Exercise is as effective as antidepressants in some cases and is an all-natural treatment to fight depression.[20] It has been scientifically proven that if you can get your heart rate up for twenty minutes a day, five days a week, you will feel better emotionally. Exercising releases endorphins, which are chemicals the body produces to relieve stress and pain. So, once you start becoming active in your house, your next step may be to get out of the house for a bike ride, walk, or a trip to the gym. Moving your body through any exercise is a medically proven method of improving the way you feel.

People who cannot be physically active may find it all the more important to keep their minds working. If you are housebound or have limited mobility, there are many ways to stimulate your mind besides watching (often mind-numbing) TV shows. There are books to read, courses to take online, cooking classes, and documentaries to watch. There are hundreds of ways to keep your mind active, even if your body won't allow you to be physically active.

Sunlight will also boost your mood. Get in the habit of spending just five to fifteen minutes each morning outside. Studies show that this helps set your internal clock. The sun also provides essential vitamin

D and boosts serotonin levels in your brain, which helps with depression.[21]

Another way to keep your mind active is to pray. Ask God for strength, peace, wisdom, and guidance. He wants us to bring all our requests to Him, and prayer is the easiest way to do that. According to Philippians 4:6, we are not to be anxious about anything, but in every situation, by prayer and with thanksgiving, we are to present our requests to God.

As mentioned earlier, we can always pray, even when we cannot physically do anything else. And even when we don't know what to pray, God hears our prayers through our thoughts and groans. As Romans 8:26 (NIV) states:

In the same way, the Spirit helps us in our weakness. We do not know what we ought to pray for, but the Spirit himself intercedes for us through wordless groans.

There have been times when I had no idea what to pray or ask God for. My heart was so broken in those times of pure anguish that I couldn't form my thoughts into a prayer. I had to trust Him and have faith that He was with me and would carry me through. I had to keep believing I would endure my crushing grief. There may be times when you can't form the words to pray, but if you keep moving, believing, and trying day by day, moment by moment, there will come a time when you see how He was and is working in your life and the lives of others. And He can and will carry you through your most difficult times.

A poem that I always loved while growing up called "Footprints" presents such a beautiful picture of God's presence whether we realize He is there or not. Although there is controversy as to who originally penned the poem, the words have inspired many and show how God's love never fails.

FOOTPRINTS

One night I dreamed a dream.
As I was walking along the beach with my Lord.
Across the dark sky flashed scenes from my life.
For each scene, I noticed two sets of footprints in the sand,
One belonging to me and one to my Lord.

After the last scene of my life flashed before me,
I looked back at the footprints in the sand.
I noticed that at many times along the path of my life,
especially at the very lowest and saddest times,
there was only one set of footprints.

This really troubled me, so I asked the Lord about it.
"Lord, you said once I decided to follow you,
You'd walk with me all the way.
But I noticed that during the saddest and most troublesome times of my life,
there was only one set of footprints.
I don't understand why, when I needed You the most, You would leave me."

He whispered, "My precious child,
I love you and will never leave you.
Never, ever, during your trials and testings.
When you saw only one set of footprints,
It was then that I carried you."

This picture of God carrying me through my most difficult times has helped me over the years. As a young girl, I made a needlepoint wall-hanging of this poem for my mom. My mom displayed it in their home from when I gave it to her until she passed away. This poem always provided me with hope. Looking back on my life, I know He has always been with me and carried me through my most difficult times. I know this because I have witnessed miraculous things in my life and the lives of others that can only result from God's divine presence.

There may be times when you think you are mentally or physically strong enough to do something, but in the midst of it, you don't feel you can complete the task. That is entirely okay, as long as you try again. And there will come a time when you can do more than you thought you could, as the Bible shows us.

After you have suffered a little while, our God, who is full of kindness through Christ, will give you His eternal glory. He personally will come and pick you up and set you firmly in place and make you stronger than ever.
1 Peter 5:10-11 (TLB)

With persistence—in getting up every day, acknowledging and understanding your emotions, trusting the healing process, with prayer and faith that you will make it through your grief—you will become stronger and reach a place of acceptance in living your life in a new way. With time, you will begin to accept and enjoy a new normal, as the next chapter discusses.

8:28

N

HOPE IN THE DARKNESS

CHAPTER 14

NEW NORMAL

How Do I Live My New Life?

You will never again be the person you were—the person who had not yet lost a child, who had never struggled with addiction, who was cancer-free, or who had never lost a home, a job, a marriage, or a family member. After going through whatever you are going through, you will be changed and unable to return to the person you once were. As you work through it, you will eventually find peace and hope for the future, so that you feel comfortable in your new normal.

After a loss and as we adjust to life again, we begin to adapt to a new way of life. You are a changed person as a result of what you experienced. As mentioned, not everyone in your life will be open to or accepting of the new you, and that's okay. Those who stick around and embrace the person you are now will help you adapt and adjust to your new way of life.

There may be new routines, limitations, and schedules to get used to, and you may want to start some new traditions, as well.

Traditions you once had may no longer be possible to carry out as a result of your unique experiences. While the natural inclination is to feel deeply saddened by this, you may experience some surprising emotions as you discover, test, and implement new traditions. Sometimes, you will find a pressing need to honor the loss in a meaningful way. You must learn how to live and cope without the person, place, or thing you are grieving over, yet you still want to honor the memory.

Especially when it's a loss of life, honoring those we love who are no longer here makes us feel good. We have an innate desire to keep those we love with us "alive" and not forgotten. Many cultures across the globe have traditions to help future generations come to know and honor their deceased family members. *Dia de los Muertos* in Mexico is a perfect and beautiful example of this—pictures of lost loved ones are displayed, along with their favorite foods and brightly colored paper decorations and flowers (the *ofrenda* or offerings to the dead). Talking about and sharing stories and memories is one of the best ways to help others know about the people who are no longer with us here on earth.

As previously mentioned in Chapter 7, the first year is often the most difficult because we have to work through all the "firsts." The day of the loss becomes the first day of the new year of firsts. From that point forward, the first Christmas, Valentine's Day, birthday, Easter, graduation, anniversary, Mother's Day, Father's Day, Thanksgiving, family portrait, vacation, or any special occasion or tradition missed throughout that year because of the loss may be difficult.

Each person has the right to handle these firsts in their own distinctive way. Just as our personalities are unique and individually complex, so are our grieving styles. We should never punish ourselves for not grieving how others want or expect us to. It is essential to respect and love yourself enough to recognize that you are dealing with your emotions as best you can.

Once again, it is important to think ahead and have a plan for the day or event. Plan how you will spend the day. Take a walk on the beach, get out of town, go to a movie, or hold a ceremony to honor the person you've lost.

Special times, events, and holiday seasons that once brought joy may now cause a further realization of loss. Since the holiday season can bring intense pain, here are some ways to start new traditions to get through these special days. Hopefully, some of these will not only honor your loved one but also heal your heart and strengthen you as you adapt to your new normal.

✧ Write a special letter, poem, or prayer about or to your loved one.

✧ Help someone in need. It is always a blessing to bless others. When we can help others through similar experiences, we always heal a little more.

✧ Visit a place that is especially meaningful to you or your loved one.

✧ Plant a tree or flower in memory of your loved one.

✧ Buy a Christmas ornament that reminds you of your loved one in some way and place it on the tree in their memory.

✧ Give a significant book, framed photo, piece of jewelry, or article of clothing of your loved one to someone special who would appreciate the memorable gift.

✧ Light a candle as a symbol to include the loved one during the holiday activities.

✧ Have the family work on a keepsake collage together (or create one yourself)!

- Step #1 – Draw a shape (cross, square, circle, triangle) or use the entire piece of paper or canvas.

- Step #2 – Add pictures or words in the four corner spaces of the cross or within the outline.

- Step #3 – Be creative! The collage can include whatever you like and is an excellent activity for all ages, using any medium you have on hand (old magazines, photographs, construction or printer paper, colored pencils, pens, paint, markers, scissors, ribbon, fabric, glitter or gemstones). Think about including the following:

  · Meaningful words that describe things the loved one taught you, unique characteristics they possessed, or a name or significant place.

  · Memorable pictures (a visual reminder of times spent with the person and activities you enjoyed together).

✧ Make a digital photo collage or video of special times. There are many online services that do this.

✧ Create a memory book with pictures, mementos, meaningful cards, drawings, anecdotes, or poems.

✧ Donate a CuddleCot to a hospital to help grieving parents of babies or a CuddleBlanket to a hospice for grieving families of older individuals.

✧ Order personalized memorial items online, such as a weighted plush animal, jewelry made of flowers or your loved one's ashes, or an engraved locket. (Several of my favorite websites can be found at www.828HOPE.com in the resource section. There are always new or local artisans to discover on Etsy or at your local Farmers' Market, who can also offer these items.)

✧ Create a family Christmas photo using a meaningful object, such as a balloon, rose, jewelry, or teddy bear to subtly honor and include the deceased family member.

✧ Donate money to a charity or cause that had special meaning to your loved one or is related to a diagnosis or cause of death for which you'd like to raise awareness.

✧ Visit the cemetery or place where you scattered ashes, whether alone or with family and friends, to place flowers, pray, journal, reminisce, and honor your loved one.

✧ Have a birthday celebration with cake. Surviving children often want to have a party on their sibling's birthday, which can be a great way to get them involved in honoring the brother or sister they lost, and it often becomes an annual tradition. When our kids were old enough to understand that they had an older brother in heaven, they requested a party for Matthew's birthday. We ended up getting a cake and sang "Happy Birthday" to Matthew. It was a sweet activity that meant something special for us all.

✧ Balloon release. A balloon release ceremony is one of the meaningful activities we share with the Empty Arms groups we lead. During the last group session, we provide white helium-filled balloons representing each baby who has died. We use white balloons to represent purity and innocence. We supply black felt-tip pens for parents to write names, meaningful words, poems, Bible verses, or special notes to their baby. Once everybody is ready to release their balloon, we stand in a circle, read a poem, and ask if anyone would like to say anything, pray, or simply speak their baby's name. We then raise our balloons in the center and release them together. The white balloons typically stay in a cluster, creating a beautiful luminescent sight against the night sky. It is a lovely visual image of our loved ones being carried up to heaven. (Note: check with local ordinances in your area before doing this, as this activity may not be allowed for environmental protection reasons.)

✧ Buy paper lanterns and light up the night sky, similar to the balloon release. (Note: again, check with local ordinances in your area before doing this, as this activity may not be allowed for environmental protection reasons.)

✧ Use a favorite T-shirt or clothes to make a quilt or stuffed animal. There are online services that do this as well.

✧ Have a canvas painting created or a photo enlargement made from a favorite picture.

✧ Ask friends and family to write a card to your loved one for a birthday or Christmas. (If the latter, you can put up a stocking for them and put the cards you receive in it to be read on Christmas morning as everyone takes turns opening their presents.)

✧ Create a social media page to honor loved ones with pictures, memories, and space for others to share. Schedule events for special dates and holidays, where others can light candles or find a unique way to honor your loved one and share. A dear friend gave beautiful shells to everyone attending her brother's memorial service and asked everyone to leave the shell at a place that was special to them or a place they thought her brother would enjoy. She then asked them to take a picture and share it with others on a Facebook page created in her brother's honor. It was amazing to see all the photos and hear many beautiful stories about where the shells were placed worldwide in honor of my friend's brother. It was healing for all involved and provided much comfort for my friend.

✧ Luminaries - Many towns, churches, garden clubs, and other organizations distribute luminaries (white bags anchored by a layer of sand, in which a white candle is lit to create a beautiful light display lining the curbside) at Christmastime. I remember driving through my sister's neighborhood in Pennsylvania during a visit with her the year before she died. It was one of the most beautiful sights our family had ever seen. For miles, street after street was lined with white candlelit bags. After my sister passed away, Rick vowed to light luminaries every Christmas to honor my sister and all the loved ones we had lost over the years. It has become a special tradition for Rick to place and light each luminary in front of our house. Once they are all lit, he gathers our family to see the beautiful luminaries lining our part of the street. It is a lovely way to remember and honor those no longer with us on Christmas Eve.

✧ Kintsugi – the Japanese art of putting broken pottery pieces back together with gold—a metaphor for healing and creating something of beauty from the broken pieces of life.

✧ Painted Rocks – During the COVID-19 pandemic quarantine, I began painting "hope" rocks. Each rock has a Bible verse written on one side and a beautiful painted design on the other side. Every day, as I would go out for my morning run in my neighborhood, I placed hope rocks in various places for people to find. That time was one of much loss and uncertainty, so I would pray a blessing for the person who found the Hope Rock—and pray that the Hope Rock would bring comfort, a smile and hope to whoever found it. As I would go out the next day, the rocks were always gone. The Hope Rocks are intended for someone who might be going through a difficult time to provide added hope. I plan to encourage those who find the Hope Rocks to take a picture and share a brief story or a unique gift that God provided that day (a call from a friend, something in nature, a song on the radio, a poem) and post it on Instagram at @828HopeInTheDarkness. There is something about sharing your story and gifts from God that is very healing and a way to help and encourage others. At some point, I would like to be able to provide the Hope Rocks in pairs so that one could be kept and the other given away, eventually amassing their own Hope Rock collections. The more you give away, the more you have. We are always blessed by being a blessing to others.

These are all ways to honor those we have loved and lost over the years, and as we now have a new normal, it may be the time to start some new traditions as you adjust to your new life. With every ending, there is a new beginning.

Therefore, if anyone is in Christ, the new creation has come:
The old has gone, the new is here!
2 Corinthians 5:17 (NIV)

8:28

E

HOPE IN THE DARKNESS

CHAPTER 15

ENDINGS LEAD TO NEW BEGINNINGS

New Beginnings

It is usually through our most difficult times that we learn and grow the most. Some of life's most significant turning points happen when we have been forced into a difficult situation. The death of our precious Matthew was the most devastating loss we could have ever imagined. In an effort to survive such loss, we turned to God, which led us to Saddleback Church. The very first service we attended introduced us to the Empty Arms ministry and we immediately signed up for the eight-week session. The support group was such a blessing to Rick and me that we decided to become leaders. Nearly three decades later, we continue to help others through their grief and losses in the Empty Arms ministry.

As much as we would love to have Matthew here, that wasn't God's plan. His plans and purposes are always much bigger and more significant than ours. He changed our hearts to help the hurting. The end of Matthew's life here on earth was a new beginning for Rick and me. Life would never be the same from that moment on. We were different people for having gone through what we went through, and our loss was the beginning of a new phase of life. It was an ending that resulted in a new beginning.

The most devastating time (when our hopes and dreams for our firstborn son ended) led and continues to lead us to more blessings than we could have ever imagined. If anyone had told me at the time of losing Matthew that we would be helping other parents through similar losses for the next thirty years and that I would write a book about helping people through loss and grief, I would have told them they were crazy! How could I possibly help others when I was in such pain and agonizing sadness?

Regardless of the tragedies that occur, whether the loss of a spouse or a job, financial loss, or a loss of health, we must all choose how to deal with the situation. It is *your* choice how you deal with whatever life throws at you. Ending a job may result in a new direction or career path for your life. Similarly, the end of one relationship will lead to new relationships, and a move or losing a home will lead to a new home and new relationships. It may not happen right away, and maybe terrifying and overwhelming to think about when it does happen, but every ending leads to a new beginning. And conversely, every new phase of life signifies the ending of a previous phase and an opportunity for growth.

Looking back at those initial years after losing our first son and joining the Empty Arms ministry, I could have never imagined the blessings we would experience as a result of our loss. The saddest time in our life has brought us some of the greatest rewards. Though I wish Matthew and our other baby could have lived, it is through them that we have been blessed to *be* a blessing to so many others going through similar losses.

We have met wonderful people and made lifelong friends as a result of our work, as our losses bind us in an indescribable way. We have shed tears of sadness and shared tears of joy in seeing couples come full circle as they bring another baby into this world. When couples come to us, most are completely broken by their grief, but over time, we can see hope and new beginnings emerge. We have witnessed the healing of emotions, bodies, and relationships.

Looking back on those early days, if someone had told me I would be leading a grief support group and helping hundreds of couples heal after losing a child, I would have said, "Nope, that doesn't sound like a life for me!" Not in my wildest dreams could I have imagined taking on such a huge task, yet as I look back, I wouldn't trade this life of helping others for anything. Yes, I would have loved to have been able to raise Matthew and watch him grow up, but my hopes and dreams weren't part of God's plan for Matthew's life. God had a much bigger plan for Matthew and all of us.

Matthew's short life has impacted more lives than many in a lifetime, and that has been a beautiful blessing to be a part of. The willingness for Rick and me to use our pain to help others was a new beginning for us. The more we have been able to help others, the more we are blessed and healed. You can't change the past, but you can change your perspective and trajectory for your future. Focus on hope for the future and look for new beginnings as a result of your past. And if you are open to using your heartbreaks to help others, you will find purpose, blessings, healing and hope in and through your past and pain to lead you to new beginnings. **Sometimes, our greatest blessings can be a result of our most significant pain.**

I've been unable to find who the author is, but the following poem is one that my mother-in-law hand-wrote in a card she sent me on Matthew's birthday a few years after he passed away. It is a beautiful reminder of God's plan as we process our losses and move into our new beginnings.

There's A Reason

> For every pain that we must bear,
> For every burden, every care –
> There's a reason

> For every grief that bows the knee,
> For every teardrop that is shed—
> There's a reason

> For every hurt, for every plight,
> For every lonely, pain-racked night –
> There's a reason

> But if we trust God as we should,
> It will all work out for our good.
> He knows the reason.

There is so much truth in this little poem. As difficult as it is to see the reason when going through a difficult time, when you reflect on the time that has passed, you may be able to see why certain things had to happen as they did.

I think about this in so many areas of my life. The pain we go through, more often than not, leads to future blessings. I think about what my life would be like had Matthew and our other baby survived. It is hard to imagine, but I also know that had things turned out differently, we likely wouldn't have had the two children that followed those losses.

I have become a better person *because* of the losses we've endured. I am more empathetic and sympathetic to others and what they are going through. When going through a profound loss, one can't help but have their perspective changed. Before my losses, things in life came pretty easy for me, but losing Matthew threw me for a loop. With such depth of pain, I understood more clearly the pain others were going through. Empathizing on this level can be a blessing and a curse because it can be very painful. I physically hurt when others hurt.

I became a new person the day I lost Matthew. His birth and death day became markers in time for me. It seemed my life was split into two distinct periods: before Matthew died and after Matthew died. We can all look at the significant times that have profoundly impacted our lives. Those significant times create markers by which we determine periods in our lives, whether happy or sad—the time before or after marriage, before or after a divorce, during addiction and since sobriety, before the loss of a loved one and after the loss.

Who we are is a product of our experiences. Reflecting on past experiences can help us see how we have been shaped into the people we are today. Each significant experience leads to a new experience, beginning, or phase of life. Though it can be painful to think back on what has happened, it is interesting to see how new beginnings evolve through past experiences.

For many people, part of choosing well and moving forward is using what they have learned from the past. If you're familiar with history and prior generations, you know that people were constantly building altars of remembrance and sharing stories of the past—at first, in an oral tradition, and later, with written records. These methods would help current and future generations learn lessons from the past, allowing them to adapt to their environments and respond to similar situations their ancestors faced. Written and oral records ensured the survival of many generations while providing a rich verbal and written history for archeological and anthropological studies many centuries later. We can all look back on our lives and think about the choices we have made. Our good or bad decisions have impacted our lives moving forward, each with their own set of consequences. Just as with cultures through the ages, the stories and past choices combine to make us who we are today.

When thinking about my story, looking back has been helpful. I remember doing a college exercise that involved writing my eulogy and thinking about how I wanted to be remembered after I died. At the time, it seemed disturbing to contemplate, but over the years, I've thought about that exercise and even more so during the time of so much loss in my family. What was a questionable writing assignment back then became a need in my adulthood with writing and delivering eulogies for the memorial services of my family members. I wanted to share about their lives, who they were to me, and how I would remember them.

There hasn't been a better catalyst for change than writing down how I'd like to be remembered. I ask myself the following questions:

Am I living the way I want to be remembered?

Am I honoring God and those I love by the way I am living?

Am I a good example?

These are questions we can all ask ourselves to keep in check with how we are living and how we will be remembered.

A Timeline

Another exercise that impacted me as much—if not more—was to write a timeline of my life in ten-year increments. I learned this valuable exercise during one of my women's Bible studies. I was to prayerfully list my milestone markers in each of those ten-year spans.

This can be a daunting and painful task. Putting pen to paper and sharing the good, bad, and the ugly wasn't easy, but every time I look back and see where I've been, where I am, and where I am going, it increases my faith to see the whole story—even the painful parts. It helps me physically see, on paper, and realize that God is in control. It is tangible, a tactile reminder of the ways in which the Lord operates behind the scenes. He is with me and always working in me. Especially through pain and disappointments, He's working. He uses our life experiences, good and bad, to shape us into who we are today.

EXERCISE 7: Create a Timeline

Write a timeline of your life in ten-year increments. Prayerfully list your milestones, creating an overview of your life.

Start with when you were born (or even in the womb). Write down anything important you remember, or stories people told you about when you were a baby. What happened that may have shaped who you are today?

Include your hurts, joys, accomplishments, and disappointments. Check off whether it was a negative experience or a positive one, and then thoughtfully consider whether any good could or did come of that experience. This is the most important part, so take your time. It can be eye-opening and life-changing when you realize that the experience you have hated all your life resulted in something positive.

Do this for each ten-year timeframe.

Timeframe	Memory	Positive?	Negative?	What good can or did come of this?
Age 0-9				
Age 10-19				
Age 20-29				

Age 30-39				
Age 40-49				
Age 50-59				
Age 60-69				
Age 70-79				
Age 80 and above				

Reflect

Look back and see where you've been, where you are now, and where you are going.

Consider what in your past may contribute to God's bigger plan for you and your loved ones.

Think about how God is working in your life.

Take a moment to pray, listen to the Lord, and ask Him to work through you. Ask Him to turn your challenges into positives and reshape your life for good. Ask Him to help you find purpose in your pain and to help you to start to see new beginnings.

Highlight the items in the positive column and those in the "what good came of it?" column.

Return to your answers periodically to challenge yourself to come up with something positive that came from each of the experiences. By acknowledging the good, you are getting one step closer to understanding God's plan for you.

As I mentioned before, thinking about life with Matthew and our other baby here on earth is bittersweet. I probably would have stopped at two children, had they lived. With that in mind, that would mean that our son, Ryan, and daughter, Avery, wouldn't be here. I know without a doubt that both Ryan and Avery are amazing gifts and living lives of significance here on earth. Ryan has traveled to Africa three times on mission trips and has worked in local community ministries and for organizations developing churches nationwide, and he married a beautiful supportive Christian woman. Avery has also been on mission trips and has worked for a company that finds jobs for people in need and is currently working with a company that develops technology and non-lethal weaponry for the military, law enforcement, and civilians and married a wonderfully supportive man. Both Ryan and Avery are living lives of significance, and both bring such joy, wisdom, and laughter into our lives and the lives of others. And should they be blessed with children, I know there is a plan and purpose for their children as well.

I trust and know that God has a much bigger and better plan for my life and my children's lives than I could ever imagine. There is a reason Ryan and Avery are here, and I can't imagine not having Ryan and Avery in our lives. Over and over again, I see God working in my life, and when difficulties arise, I know I must trust in His plan, not mine. We must try not to fear painful endings because every ending leads to a new beginning.

I know that God holds to His promise in Romans 8:28, *"And we know that in all things God works for the good of those who love him, who have been called according to his purpose."* It can take time to get there, but I believe if we listen to God and are willing to have Him work through us, He will turn our challenges into something positive. Rather than making excuses or blaming others for our circumstances, remember that God can reshape our lives for good.

The next chapter shares stories that exemplify such hope. If we are open to God using our experiences, we can honor those we love and find purpose in our pain. I am hopeful that some of these stories will provide you with encouragement for the future. They are stories of love, loss, persistence, healing, compassion, strength, faith, grace, and survival. Stories from people who bravely used their losses, experiences, and personal dark times to transform their lives and the lives of others—examples of how endings miraculously and gradually created a space for new beloved beginnings.

8:28

S

HOPE IN THE DARKNESS

CHAPTER 16

STORIES OF SURVIVAL AND HOPE

Stories of Pain and Purpose

When we feel everything is out of our control, consider this Bible passage, remembering that we can handle whatever we are dealing with.

> *Dear brothers and sisters, when troubles of any kind come your way, consider it an opportunity for great joy. For you know that when your faith is tested, your endurance has a chance to grow. So let it grow, for when your endurance is fully developed, you will be perfect and complete, needing nothing. If you need wisdom, ask our generous God, and he will give it to you. He will not rebuke you for asking. But when you ask him, be sure that your faith is in God alone. Do not waver, for a person with divided loyalty is as unsettled as a wave of the sea that is blown and tossed by the wind. Such people should not expect to receive anything from the Lord. Their loyalty is divided between God and the world, and they are unstable in everything they do.*
> *James 1: 2–8 (NLT)*

When faced with a decision, seek guidance from God to help you choose the right path. Be receptive to His support and have faith that

He will grant you the knowledge and wisdom you need to move forward. The stories that follow are personal accounts from people who transformed their difficult situations into fresh starts and utilized their painful experiences for a greater purpose. These individuals placed their trust in God to find meaning and purpose through their pain.

Marcella Johnson – Founder THE COMFORT CUB (501 C3 Non-profit)

I never thought I would ever be able to honestly say that losing my son, Baby George, could be one of the greatest blessings in my life. Please know I did not come to this right away. Losing George was absolutely the darkest time of my life. I was so depressed and felt like I wanted to die too. I had just given birth and all I wanted was to be with my baby, wherever he was. But just where was he?

As a Christian, I have always been taught that when you die, you go to heaven. But where is heaven and how do you get there? I needed to know more about this place and through this quest, I learned that heaven is real. I also learned how important it is to place God at the center of your life. Before this experience, I believed in God, but I never knew Him personally.

It all started when I was six months pregnant. At that time, I received the diagnosis that the sweet baby boy I was carrying had a life-threatening disease. I was told he could die any day, or if I were lucky enough to make it to term, he would die during the birthing process. The best-case scenario was that he would be born alive and die shortly thereafter. By the grace of God and against all odds, he was born alive. I was able to hold him, hug him, and tell him that I loved him. He died that same day in my arms. It was the saddest moment of my life and yet it was so full of grace and beauty.

When George came into the world, I felt a glorious presence enter with him that filled the room with love and light. And when he passed, I felt that presence leave with him. His heart had stopped, and the doctor pronounced his death.

Along with the obvious emotional pain you would expect after losing a child, I also experienced some very strange physical pain. My heart literally felt like it was breaking. The pain in my chest was so real and continual. I had trouble taking a full breath, and I felt like I had an open wound in my chest. The only thing that helped was to apply pressure over my heart, just as you would with an open wound. And not only that, but my arms ached badly, and no amount of rubbing, massaging, lotions, or anything could make it go away.

It was not until I visited my son's grave that I found any kind of relief. I had asked my dad to join me. I was feeling so sad that I did not want to be alone. He arrived before I did and found a beautiful terra-cotta pot full of flowers waiting at the grave. My father insisted that I take this lovely pot of flowers home with me, but I really couldn't have cared less about it. I was so heartbroken that I did not even want to speak. However, he was so insistent that I had to take it from him just to get him to stop talking to me!

Much to my surprise, the moment I got that pot in my arms, the aching in my heart and arms vanished completely. After I left, I found myself not wanting to put that pot down, so I ended up carrying it all around my house for comfort. I thought I had surely lost my mind.

However, I later read that it's common for women to seek weighted objects for relief after losing a child. I read about women who carried around five-pound sacks of flour, heavy pillows, or vases. But the case that really touched me was when I read about a first-time mom who lost her tiny baby. She went to the grocery store and found a pineapple the exact length and weight of her baby. She brought it home, wrapped it in one of her baby's blankets, and sat in the rocking chair, rocking her pineapple like she would have rocked her baby. Sure, she might sound crazy to those who can't relate to this loss. But after having lived it, I understood this woman's great pain and just how desperate she was to do whatever she could to bring herself out of her suffering.

After reading this, I felt a heavenly call on my heart to create something that could help these women. My hope was that no other mother would ever have to leave the hospital empty-handed after losing a child the way I did. It was the loneliest walk of my life. I wanted to give them something to hold to fill their empty arms and to let them know they were not alone in this difficult journey. That is when I came up with the idea of creating a weighted therapeutic teddy bear called The Comfort Cub.

At first, I made the teddy bears by hand and filled them with split peas to give them their heft. I gave them all a purple bow because I could not afford to do half of them in pink and half of them in blue. So, I put the two colors together and came up with purple as it was a gender-neutral color. I also secretly liked it because purple is the color of royalty and a symbol of our Lord Jesus Christ.

My faith is at the center of my work. I do not know what caused this undeni-able desire to try to make the journey a little easier for the next woman who would certainly come after me. I wanted to give back what I had been given. I wanted to provide hope and comfort. I saw a deep need that I felt the Lord had asked me to try to help fill.

Although we started out just for women, we have now found that The Comfort Cub provides profound relief in all kinds of trauma situations. We work with police departments on accidents, suicides, car crashes, and mass shootings. The response that some people have experienced from holding The Comfort Cub seems miraculous to me. I believe the love and comfort that people feel during their time of trauma is so much greater than anything I or any other human could ever share. I truly believe that when they hug, hold, or sleep with The Comfort Cub, it is the love of God they are feeling. This little bear of hope and healing comes from Him, and He seems to have given it a life of its own. My goal is to let others know that they are not alone in their experiences of deep loss and sadness. That they will find a way to rise again and carry on. I want them to know that they will get through this hardship, too. But I also know that I could never have gotten through this without my faith in God. Without His goodness, without Him holding me up when I could barely breathe, I never would have made it. I hope that The Comfort Cub helps people know they will survive, too.

Roger Crawford – Author | Motivational Speaker

On October 1960, my mother felt the contractions that signaled my impending arrival. Accompanied by my father, also named Roger, she went to the hospital—a place where, during that era, fathers weren't allowed in the delivery room. Instead of having my father restlessly walk the corridors, hospital staff advised him to go home and wait for their call.

Anesthesia during labor was common back then, so my mother was not conscious when I came into the world. Before allowing her to see me, the doctors chose to prepare her emotionally and called my father. When he arrived, his no-nonsense demeanor took charge; he wanted to see me first and deal with the details later.

No parent ever expects to face the reality that awaited them: I was born with just two fingers on my left forearm and one on my right. My left leg was noticeably shorter, and its foot had only two toes. The knee was misaligned, offering no stability. But fortunately, my right leg was functional, albeit with a narrow foot and three toes.

Discussing this experience in retrospect, my admiration for my parents' fortitude is boundless. The societal outlook on disabilities was still in its infancy in 1960.

Their concerns about my future intensified when they heard the daunting prognosis from the doctor: "I don't believe your son will ever walk."

With their encouragement, not only did I learn to walk, but I also became an NCAA Division One Hall of Fame Athlete, mastering the ability to outperform able-bodied competitors. This journey earned me the revered ITA Achievement Award, granted by the International Tennis Hall of Fame.

The question I often get is, "How did you overcome your disability?" My response is straightforward: Disability isn't something you "overcome." It's about adjusting, relinquishing control over what's out of your hands, and cultivating acceptance. My faith was the cornerstone of this transformation.

If you ever find yourself bogged down by life's hurdles, consider leaning into a higher power. Let go of your ego; elevate your spirit by focusing on divine perspectives. By doing so, you don't just diminish the weight of your troubles; you empower yourself to rise above them.

Our true limitations surface when we attempt to take control, rarely venturing beyond what we can personally accomplish. Put faith in a greater strength and watch the insurmountable turn manageable.

Today, as an author and a professional speaker, I've had the honor of inspiring over 4,000 audiences globally. I also host a weekly TV show, "Motivational Mondays with Roger Crawford." My journey illustrates how faith can transform what the world deems a 'burden' into an unparalleled 'blessing.'

Veronica Valli – Recovery Coach | Award-winning Author of Soberful | Podcaster: Soberful

I think there are two ways you can become an alcoholic. I think you're either born that way or you simply need to drink enough alcohol and become one.

I believe I was born an alcoholic. I believe this because I've always felt "different." My earliest memories are of feeling "odd," and "uncomfortable in my own skin." I felt like I was looking out at the world through a glass screen; I was on one side, and everyone else was on the other.I felt separate, alone, unconnected. It didn't seem to matter what I did; I never felt like I truly "fit in" or "belonged" anywhere. These feelings began long before I ever tried alcohol.

When I finally tried alcohol at around fifteen, it felt like a light bulb went on. All of a sudden, I felt complete; I felt "right," and I had confidence and belief in myself.

Drinking did something to me; it made me feel normal. *I never drank "normally," whatever that is. I drank alcoholically from the word go. I could never get enough of this substance that made me feel so good.*

For two years, I really, really enjoyed taking drugs and getting drunk. I had a great time, and then, at age seventeen, everything went horribly wrong.

I had taken some LSD and had a "bad trip." This had never happened before, and I didn't know how to handle it. I felt panicky and scared. I was seeing and hearing things and got very paranoid. The feeling of terror grew, and even when I began to "come down," the fear and panic didn't leave; they got worse. I now know that I went into drug-induced psychosis, but at the time, I had no idea what was happening to me. The worst thing was I couldn't tell anyone around me how I felt. I put on a "mask" and pretended everything was okay. I was terrified of anyone finding out what was happening; I became imprisoned by my fear.

Every day of living was agony for me, and I didn't know how to carry on.

This went on for months. I didn't have the words to express what was happening. I couldn't even begin to articulate what I was experiencing. I was too scared to say it out loud because if I did, it meant what was happening to me was real. I was still clinging to the hope that one day, I would wake up and be normal again.

The next ten years of my life, from seventeen to twenty-seven, were a living hell. I was never, ever free from fear; it was the overwhelming emotion I woke up to every morning. Some days, I felt like I could hardly breathe for the sheer terror of having to get through the day and pretend to be normal.

At seventeen, my drinking shifted from "having fun" to using it to cope with how I felt. I knew there was something very wrong with me; I just didn't know what. I did try to get help. I looked everywhere. I went to doctors, counselors, psychiatrists, psychologists, therapists, and churches—anywhere that offered some kind of hope. I was treated for anxiety or depression but never my alcoholism. The truth is, I either lied about how much I drank, or I was never asked. No one ever picked up on the fact that drinking was my real problem. Whatever treatment I was offered only gave me a reprieve so, inevitably, I would revert to familiar feelings of loneliness, isolation, despair, and discontent. Drinking always gave me temporary relief from these feelings.

I tried every method known to alcoholics to try and "fix" my life. It is amusing to me now to see how unoriginal I was in my attempts to try and make things "better." Every alcoholic or addict I've known has tried the same methods.

Throughout my twenties, I drank heavily—more than I knew was good for me. I always sought a peer group that drank as much as I did. I drank before any social situation because I was too scared to face people. I drank before parties because I was scared there wouldn't be enough booze for me to get the "buzz" I needed. I drank anytime I felt scared and couldn't cope. Toward the end of my drinking, I began to sneak drinks and drink on my own; I preferred that to sharing my booze.

In my mid-twenties, I started using cocaine whenever I drank because it enabled me to drink more. However, cocaine gave me the worst "come downs" ever. I was suicidal. I would wake up the next day and feel as if my soul had been scraped out and was lying on the floor next to me. I didn't know how I was going to get out of bed, let alone make it through the rest of my life. My feelings of loneliness and despair intensified.

I never actually became physically dependent on alcohol. I could always go for some time without it. Usually, I would switch to something else—such as prescription drugs, pot, or anything that could help me get through the day. I've known the shame and degradation of being a female alcoholic and sleeping with men I didn't like, just to feel wanted. I've never been arrested, bankrupt, or fired, or any of the other terrible things that often happen to alcoholics. At first, I thought I couldn't be an alcoholic because I wasn't somehow "qualified," but I learned that it isn't the drinking and consequences that make you an alcoholic; it's the thoughts and feelings that drive alcoholism. It was then that I finally understood what my problem was.

As soon as I understood the problem, I could then embark on the solution.

I got help from experts who understood alcoholism and I joined a self-help group. For the first time in my life, I realized I wasn't alone. It was through a self-help program that I found God.

Getting clean and sober was the hardest thing I have ever done, but there was no choice for me; I couldn't go back to how I was living. I so wanted to live, to make my life count, and to see what I was capable of. When I got sober, these things, at last, became possible.

Finally, I became free of the prison I had made for myself; the only thing that had ever limited me was my thinking. Recovery gave me a new perspective on life; it gave me back my self-belief and confidence. I am finally engaging in the process of reaching my full potential and becoming the woman I was meant to be. I no longer have a 50-percent life of just getting by, just coping. I am no longer scared; I am just the opposite; I am fearless in everything I do. I no longer worry whether you like me or not, because I love who I am. I wake up every day and find something to be joyful about. Yes, my life still offers challenges, but none of them threaten to capsize me as they used to. I relish challenges, and I can now learn, grow, and become the best version of myself I'm capable of being.

Life is a beautiful adventure now instead of a scary, threatening place. I live a life now beyond anything I could have dreamed of before. I am on fire with the possibilities there are in front of me.

I have now been sober for over twenty years. I became a wife and mother, found a career as a psychotherapist, wrote three books on how to recover from an alcohol problem and also host a podcast called "Soberful." The best thing of all is that I get to help other people recover and live their best lives, too.

Veronica Valli author of "Soberful: uncover a sustainable fulfilling life free of alcohol."

Erick Alvarez – Entrepreneur | The Tiny House Society | Motivational Speaker

I didn't know what love was. I was born to an alcohol-and-drug-addicted single mother; my father walked away before I was born, and never returned. Before my first birthday, my mother left me with relatives and drank herself away. I was placed into foster care at six years of age and spent my childhood living in many homes—feeling discouraged, angry, and alone. I didn't know what love was; however, I fully understood what love was not. I knew love wouldn't abandon me. I knew love wouldn't hurt me. I knew love wouldn't give up on me.

I didn't know what a relationship was. When I was twelve years old, my mother managed her addictions long enough for a child welfare judge to give her custody of me. My mother gave me a twin bed in the corner of her bedroom. Sometimes, we lived in a motel room; sometimes, we lived in a month-to-month room rental. In only four years of living with my mother, I received black eyes from her high heels, bruises from heavy objects (such as heaters) thrown at me, and bloody wounds from cord and cable beatings. Some days were more difficult than others, especially those days when my mother would scream without hesitation:

✧ "You're punishment for all the sins I've committed!"

✧ "I wish you had never been born."

✧ "No one will ever take the shirt off their back and give it to you."

Sometimes, my mother would grab a used toilet brush and scrub it against my mouth or force me to lay on the kitchen floor while she stepped on my face. Although my mother was physically, verbally, and emotionally abusive, my heart's only desire was to be loved as her son. On the days when punishments seemed unbearable, I would distract myself from my pain by imagining that one day, when I least expected it, my mom would appear with arms wide open, tears in her eyes and a smile that radiated love—and she would say something like, "I found you! I'm sorry you had to live with a mother who hurt you for so long. I am your mom—and I love you."

I never pretended that my mother didn't exist. On the contrary, even through the beatings and humiliation, I always believed my mother was the most beautiful woman to ever walk on Earth and that her smile could bring life to anything. She was the wisest person I knew; she was so wise that she would tell me things like:

✧ *"Erick, this is not a family—this is not what loving families are like. It is your responsibility to figure out one day what a loving family looks like, and it's your responsibility to have a loving family of your own."*

✧ *"You won't be living here when you're eighteen; you'll be on your own sooner than you think. When you're on your own, leave the bad experiences and all the hurt I have caused behind, and take only the good experiences, the wisdom you've learned. No one else is responsible for the outcome of your life but you."*

I was sixteen the day my mother kicked me in the back, beat me until I bled, clawed my shirt to pieces, and told me to leave her house and never return. I didn't have a wallet, a cell phone, or a shirt. I walked to a neighbor's house and asked if I could use their phone. They welcomed me inside, gave me one of their son's shirts to wear, and led me to a room where I could use a phone. But before cleaning my blood, before wiping away my tears, and before making a call, I knelt beside a bed and prayed a simple prayer that I have been praying ever since: "God, every step I take from here on out, I will take toward You."

I have learned that it is my responsibility to ask for advice when I don't understand relationships, to ask for forgiveness when I damage a relationship, to desire and seek healthy relationships, and to be authentic and genuine every day in each relationship I have.

Even though I never met my biological father, I know my dad loves me. Even though I never had a loving relationship with my biological mother, I know my mom loves me. I've always believed that my dad and mom loved me more than I could possibly understand. I was seventeen the first time I cried, yelled, and screamed to God that I needed a dad and a mom. It took me about a year to realize that I could call God my mom and my dad. He was and is fully there for me. He would love me, nurture me, and never give up on me.

That same year, I found a forever family who welcomed me into their home unconditionally and gave me unlimited hope. A woman named Karen became my mom, and a man named Rick became my Dad. The Hacker family gave me a bed to sleep on, without knowing anything about my past. I was allowed to eat anything I wanted from the pantry, and was even allowed to hide food in my dresser because it made me feel safe. At eighteen, for the very first time in my life, I had a packed lunch with three Oreo cookies in it. And I was eighteen when someone believed that I could go to college—without having a nickel to my name. I was eighteen when I celebrated Christmas for the first time—with a forever family. God's love has always overflowed from them and given me faith to go on. God has taught me that family isn't about biological relations, last name, or looks. Family is about unconditional love and unlimited hope.

Year after year, God has taught me that love is a choice, a daily decision to make, a commitment. I've learned that true love is unconditional and abundant. I believe love and relationships are not momentary things that happen from time to time, but they are both processes to which I must re-commit daily by demonstrating love through actions. I've learned that when you love someone, you are delighted to serve them. I've learned that unconditional love begins not by thinking less of yourself, but simply thinking of yourself less. I have learned that relationships are continually developing and growing over time. Relationships are organic, authentic, genuine, vulnerable, transparent, forgiving, and selfless.

I have much more to learn about love and relationships; however, I'm excited to learn from the relationship I love the most: my relationship with God. God has shown me love in deep and amazing ways. He uses every person in my life as an example, a light, or a vessel to communicate His unconditional love to me. Since I have begun to learn about love through experiencing it, I hope that I can prove my biological mother to be as wise as I once thought she was. I hope to live out the love I have learned through having a loving family of my own.

In the midst of my difficult experiences, I clung to the belief that there was a purpose to my life, and a higher plan that I couldn't fully comprehend at the time. I embraced Romans 8:28, a verse that states, "And we know that in all things God works for the good of those who love him, who have been called according to his purpose," and began to see the transformative power of my hardships. These trials, as challenging as they were, became the foundation upon which I built my resilience, empathy, and determination. Today, I stand as a testament to the incredible ways in which adversity can shape a person for the better. A verse that also resonated deeply within my soul was James 1:27: "Religion that God our Father accepts as pure and faultless is this: to look after orphans and widows in their distress and to keep oneself from being polluted by the world." This scripture became a guiding light, shaping my perspective and fueling my determination to transform adversity into a force for good.

One of the ways I turned my difficult past into positive change was through my involvement with Royal Family Kids Camp, an organization dedicated to helping children in the Foster Care System across the United States. Drawing upon my own experiences, I became a beacon of hope and understanding for these children, offering them a listening ear and a shoulder to lean on. In their eyes, I saw reflections of my own struggles, and in their smiles, I witnessed the resilience that can emerge from the depths of despair. My own journey became a source of hope and understanding, allowing me to be a pillar of support, offering them genuine understanding, compassion, and an unwavering belief that their past did not define their future. Through this work, I discovered the healing power of empathy, and how my own journey could serve as a source of strength for others facing similar struggles.

Additionally, I embraced my entrepreneurial spirit and founded Tiny House Society, a company rooted in the principles of James 1:27 and aimed at assisting people in finding affordable Tiny Homes on Wheels My own experiences with unstable living situations fueled my passion to provide others with a sense of security and stability. Through Tiny House Society, I hope to empower individuals and families to create homes filled with love and warmth, where love and acceptance flourishes, irrespective of past hardships and regardless of their past circumstances. My own experiences with unstable living situations fuels my passion to provide others with a sense of security and stability.

Looking back, I recognize that the difficulties I endured equipped me with the resilience needed to overcome challenges and the compassion to help others do the same. My journey from a broken past to a promising future is a testament to the transformative power of faith, perseverance, and love. Throughout my journey, I have not walked alone but alongside incredible individuals and families whose un-wavering support has been my foundation. They have stood by me through thick and thin, guiding me with their wisdom and love. Today, as I reflect on my path, I am profoundly thankful for each of them. Their presence in my life has made me stronger and more compassionate.

Rechelle Conde-Nau – Postcaster: Unabashed You | Author of Standing Tall – A Collecton of Mourning

Ninety-two days. That is how long we had with our son, Christian, before was born with a severe heart defect. His underdeveloped heart had been discovered in utero and we were told that our child would not live much past birth. My husband, Ron, and I chose to trust in God's plan for our lives and to celebrate the pregnancy, as this would be our only time with him. But he lived for ninety-two days. A gift.

Oh, there was definitely grief, tears, and long periods of pain. I still cannot hear the song from the movie Titanic *("My Heart Will Go On") without feeling a pit develop in my stomach and wanting to run to the nearest cave (and where might that be?) to wail in private. Yet through it all, we somehow did not ask why. We could have, and God would have been fine with the question, but we didn't. I cannot fully explain why.*

What about when a gift keeps on giving long after he is gone? It's what I came to know in real life in real-time. I absolutely clung to the promise of Romans 8:28: *"For we know that God causes all things to work for good to those who love him and to those who are called according to his purpose." It became my life-preserver. I began to look for the promise of that verse.*

I wanted to see the good. I hoped for it. I even expected it. Isn't that what a promise is?

Something you can count on? I knew God would not disappoint. As time went on, I began to intentionally look for the ways God worked this for good. I was asked to share a chapter of my story at a women's event, so I chose to speak about the promise of 8:28 in my life through our time with Christian. I turned around, looked back, traced events and people, and saw all the ways He blessed us—all the good.

I created a visual image of what I had discovered. A tree with Christ at the roots, the verse of Romans 8:28 *on the trunk, followed by a picture of Christian.*

Then, the branches were filled with fruit. God used this verse and worked through Christian to produce abundant fruit. The good.

Here is a partial list of the fruit—the blessings:

✧ **Reunited**. *We reconnected with three other couples who were there for us in our pain. One member from each pair went to the same high school. One of the couples had a son with the same condition ours did, so they understood our grief. They are active in grief counseling because they get it.*

✧ **Dogs**. *We got a golden retriever puppy. She helped me heal in ways I cannot fully articulate. Six months after she died, we got another one. Oh, the joy!*

✧ **Passion discovered**. *Neighbors gave us tickets to a children's theater production that came in a sympathy card. At the play, one of our kids announced, "That's what I want to do." He did and does, unto this very day. He found his passion.*

✧ **New calling**. *After being a classroom teacher for years, I shared with God that I'd love to do something with kids and theater. Two weeks later, I was offered a job to develop introductory performing arts programs to take to schools across the county. I worked there and loved it for fifteen years.*

✧ **Movie friend**. *One of the moms at the school I had taught at reached out, and we became lifelong friends. For years, we went to the movies every week and had lunch together, talking over what we'd seen and telling each other what was going on in our lives.*

✧ **Dance is fun**. *I also connected with a different friend, who reminded me how much we both wanted to tap dance. So, we did! We were even in a few recitals, and we had a blast.*

✧ **Standing Tall – A Collection of Mourning**. *I wrote a book, a collection, really, of the feelings and events after losing Christian. It contains many letters and words of wisdom from others. Their words were soothing for my heart. The book is used in that grief counseling course mentioned above.*

✧ **One more**. *My brother-in-law and his wife thought someone was missing from our extended family, so they had one more child. Grace.*

✧ **Music**. *That same brother-in-law composed a beautiful piece of music entitled "CJ," (Christian John) after our Christian, the son we lost. It is beautiful, haunting, and very special to us.*

✧ ***Prayer.*** *A close friend asked if she could put me in touch with a woman she knew who was carrying a baby who would not live much past birth. I, of course, said yes and was happy to be there for her. That same woman then started a prayer group, and we've been going strong for twenty years and counting!*

✧ ***A daughter.*** *One of the best gifts was the blessing we had of adopting a baby girl three years after Christian died. It was a dream come true. She completed our family, and I cannot imagine my life without her. I believe Christian's passing made a way for her to come to us. I can't explain God's strategy or timing on this, but I trust it. Endless love. One of the couples we know could not have biological children. One member of the couple did not want to adopt, while the other one did. They were at a stalemate, until the husband spent time with our adoptive daughter when she was a baby and fell in love with her. They soon adopted their daughter. Happy ending!*

✧ ***Podcasting. Unabashed You. How did it start?*** *It started with a quote, "And the day came when the risk to remain tight in the bud was more painful than the risk it took to blossom" Anais Nin. I knew it was intended for me at this time, and in this place. I didn't want fear to stop me from stepping out of my comfort zone. I had something inside that needed to get out, and I knew it had to do with encouraging others.*

I noticed many people struggling to feel good about who they were including at times, myself. I wanted to speak into this by creating conversation around it. I needed to show up authentic, transparent and vulnerable, while emboldening others to do the same. Through getting to know each other, and hearing stories, we can discover and expand our understanding of who we are so we can be that, fully.

Even if only my family and close friends listened it would be woefully worthwhile. It has been that and more. Unabashed You was born from this desire. It's a movement, a podcast & blog, to support being who you are without apology. These conversations will help you think, celebrate who you are, and move you in some way. Listen, read and be inspired by the guests who share in a playful get-to-know-you segment followed by a deeper-dive. There are no wrong answers. There is only you, and how you can expand in your own skin to become who you already are.

I do believe there are divine signs and messages in our everyday lives and that, if we don't open ourselves up to them, we can easily miss them. When I spoke to the

173

women that day at our event, I challenged them to find the good that comes from hard situations. It's there. Sometimes, you have to dig. Sometimes, you have to wait a while to see it, but I promise it's there. Just like in Romans 8:28.

Brian Thompson LMFT – Impact Recovery & Psychotherapy
Chasing His Light To Live His Life

> *It was a dark and stormy night.*
> *Suddenly a shot rang out!*
> *A door slammed.*
> *The maid screamed.*
> *Suddenly, a pirate ship appeared on the horizon.*
> *Snoopy (Charles M. Schultz)*

As a young child, these were my initial words of fear and darkness. As Snoopy sat on top of his doghouse and typed these first words of his novel, the animation behind him was dark, stormy, and uncertain, much like the words he was describing. I always knew that Snoopy was going to be safe and that the storms illustrated behind him were never going to hurt him or lead him away from the things in life that made him happy. As a child, this is what we want for ourselves: an innocence in our belief that everything is going to be okay. A belief that there is no monster under the bed, that nothing went bump in the night, and that evil did not roam the streets concealed in darkness.

I was born in the Midwest and for me, the idea of the hardships and pains of life seemed to be non-existent; after all, we always had the Superfriends to protect us. I went to church every week with my mom and dad and enjoyed the concept of the Lord as it seemed to fit in my fantasy world of superheroes and animated dogs. I remember thinking about church on Christmas Eve and how desperately I wanted the service to end so that Santa Claus could come to my house and spoil me. Life was great! I had my mom, my dad, friends, and family and I had not one real care in the world.

When I was four, I experienced loss for the first time. My grandfather on my mom's side of the family had a sudden heart attack at work and did not make it to the hospital. I remember my mom taking me to a neighbor's house to play with my friend. All I can remember anyone telling me is that grandpa was gone, and I would see him again someday. I remember my mom crying and being sad. There was a funeral, but I didn't attend. I remember going to the building my grandfather owned and playing around while my mom and her siblings gathered his belongings, as strange people kept coming by to take materials from the shop. It wasn't long after that my family decided to move to California. There was no discussion about grandpa; he was just gone.

Being a young child, I never really asked where grandpa was or why he left. A couple of years later, I began to understand the idea of death and what it meant for me spiritually, and I didn't like any of it. I vividly remember finding out my great aunt had passed away and I was very mad that everyone wasn't as sad as I was, even though we weren't very close. To me, death was the worst thing in the world, and I was terrified and angry. I had no idea at age seven that there were many more obstacles in life that I would need to overcome to be the person that I was meant to be.

My father was an alcoholic. He was, at times, a very physically and verbally abusive alcoholic. Often, my mom and I would "forget" to tell my father about things happening at school so that he wouldn't attend. I wanted him to love me and somehow deduced that his anger and drinking was my fault. I started playing baseball, for him, in second grade and continued well into college. Up until my ninth-grade year, he would come for an inning here or there but would always need to leave for "work." Looking back, I guess I didn't understand that, as an electrical contractor, there are many electrical emergencies that need to be addressed after six pm. My mom was always there. She would do everything she could, sometimes to her own detriment, to shield me from the darkness of my father's moods and abuse. We stuck together and although my father was suffering, and despite the occasional bruises, I was still okay.

Things from there continued to unravel. During the summer leading up to ninth grade, my baseball coach molested me. This was an occurrence that continued quite often over the next four years of my life. My own addiction was just starting to grow as alcohol went from an occasional weekend venture to an almost daily endeavor. My grades began to slip. I would stay out and not come home for a day or two, failing to tell my mom where I was or that I was okay. My dad became more abusive, and my parent's relationship was slipping away. My moral compass no longer guided me, and I did more of what I wanted rather than what I needed. God was no longer a thought in all that I was doing. I never once made an association between all that was going wrong with my life and the lack of a relationship with God.

As I approached graduation, my dad threw me out of the house. He also suggested that my mom leave, as well; she did, and movers arrived the next day taking most of what we had with us. We went to stay with a family friend, and while we were physically safe, we were both hurting. My addiction to alcohol was growing and I was not there for my mom the way I could have been. I did not apply to any colleges, instead choosing to try a junior college. This decision would lead to more destruction, take me down pathways and introduce me to people I would have never once considered, putting me further away from my mom, my former friends, and any form of a belief system.

Darkness clouded my twenties. Alcohol was no longer enough, so I graduated into using cocaine almost daily. I was able to maintain a good-paying job for many years, but that, too, fell apart. I used my savings, retirement plans, and my mom's love to pay bills and support my addictions. I had a period of homelessness where I chose to live on the streets rather than make a change. My new "friends" supported my addiction and happily took advantage of my generosity. I would call my mom on occasion as the guilt would often creep in because I knew what I was doing was killing us both. She would stay strong and not cry, but I knew how much I was hurting her. She, like always, was the only person who would talk to me. She was the only person who believed in me, even when I didn't. Occasionally, I would pray. I would babble on and on to God about how I wanted to change and how I needed all this pain to go away, but He knew I wasn't ready. I knew that, as well, but knowing that He was there, even if I wasn't ready, gave me hope.

Circumstances and many situations—too many to detail—eventually gave me the push that I needed to make a change. This was a very difficult period for me in starting to get sober and trying to put my life back on track. Much like my addiction, I felt as if I were the only person who could make this change, and did not fully turn things over to God. Ironically, I met the therapist that I credit with helping me endure these very difficult changes at the former Crystal Cathedral. I attended sessions on the church campus, and I went to the Chapel in the Sky after each meeting for a few moments of peace. It took a great deal of time before I decided to allow God to be a part of my recovery. As I look back, this was the true darkness of my life. Here I was, a thirty-year-old starting from scratch, and I failed to understand the power of the Lord and all the blessings that were at my fingertips.

I remember eventually working on my relationship with God in my third year of therapy. I discovered that I was very angry at Him, and I blamed Him for so much that had gone wrong in my life, including my dad's drinking and abusive nature, my parent's divorce, my molestation, my addiction, and many other things. I had a very hard time understanding why He allowed all these things to happen to me. Eventually, I came to terms with it all, fully accepting my role in each situation.

I realized that my relationship with God was not one of distance, but was one in which I could grow, prosper, and feel the security of His love. At the urging of my therapist, I went back to school to pursue a career in mental health, as I realized that all the things I experienced and eventually conquered would help me help others. It was difficult to start over in my thirties, but I picked up momentum, and as my relationship with God became stronger, so did my resolve to be a vessel for His word for others.

Over the past twenty years, the relationship that I have with God has changed. There are times when I am fully invested, and I feel as if I am surrounded by His love. There are times when I find myself believing that I am once again in full control of everything and that my relationship with Him can be put on the back burner. There are also times in which I find myself distant, maybe angry, or even afraid of God. These changes often lead to new levels of darkness in which I question what I am doing and whether these are the things in life that I should be pursuing.

Darkness and a lack of hope generally cloud my relationship with God, especially when it comes to the idea of death and the thoughts of losing someone important to me. Like many, I find myself in times of impending loss, praying heavily, asking that I not endure the deep sadness and pain associated with death.

Recently, however, I have experienced two major losses in my life that I am still—even after significant time has passed—struggling to overcome, losses that I am still negotiating within myself and with God.

At the beginning of 2020, I lost my best friend to his addiction to alcohol. I knew this result was always a possibility, but I believed that God would help my friend make the changes that he made in me. I wasn't angry with God, but I didn't understand why He needed to take my friend away. Over the next few weeks, I could see things from God that helped me find peace—things that only He could give me. Many of those signs and comforts guided me through the darkness of my loss and my hope for healing. Regardless of how hard, I knew that I would be okay.

In 2021, I lost another key member of my support system, as one of my Siberian Huskies passed away. I had dogs pass prior to this loss due to canine cancer, but this loss was exceptionally hard. Almost four years prior, she had been diagnosed with liver disease. At nine years of age, I elected to not put her through an extensive and very painful surgery. Instead, I continued to do all that I could to ensure the best health options and to fill her with my love. I prayed very hard every day and, at times, felt desperate for God to not take her from me. In the last few days of her life, I was aware that she was going to leave me. When it was very clear that she *had arrived at the end of her life, I was angry that He would not just bring her home to be with Him and the others. God was really in a no-win situation with me. Eventually, she left me after almost fourteen years. I was hurting and yet, I somehow knew everything was going to be okay.*

While I am still working through the most recent losses and missing them both every day, it is because of God and His gifts of faith and hope that make a huge difference in my ability to move forward. When going through my addiction, I knew that God was always there, but I chose to keep Him at a distance, so that I could do things my way. As I look back, I can see just how God kept me safe and prevented horrible things from happening to me as a result of my reckless behavior. I can look back and see how having faith in His plan has propelled me into a career as a therapist, in which my life experiences help me guide others through their own pain and suffering. I can also see how God has helped me travel through the roller coaster of emotions that I experience as a result of loss, still knowing that I will be okay again.

For me, God has been my answer. He has given me so much more in my life than I ever thought possible. It is because of Him that I have been able to progress through dark times. It is because of the hope and faith that I have in Him that I am able to support others regardless of their own personal belief systems, while still believing that He has so many more victories in store for me.

While the things I experience today do not compare to the pain and suffering I experienced in my past, I know that it takes a great force to keep me where I am. It would be easy to lose hope. It would be easy to fall back into the darkness of my addiction and sadness. I know that I will have bad days. I know that I will have losses far greater than those I have already experienced. I do not look forward to those days at all. I know that I will be very angry at God, but I also know that He will pull me up and make me stronger. I have faith, and with faith, there is hope. It's been a predominant pattern in my life. No need to change now. He will be there, as always, to love me and fill me with hope.

Terra Prickett – Founder 501C3 non profit Gloves for Grief: Punching our Pain into Purpose

If you were to tell me a year ago that I would be in a place where I could share my story like this, I would have never believed you.

Last year, I was a woman who saw no hope, felt alone, and felt misunderstood. I was completely unaware of how my loss would reshape me in a way I never imagined.

The only way to accurately explain where I am today and the journey it took to get here is to go back. When you experience the greatest pain of your life, you can clearly define the "then" and the "now." I look at photos of me before my loss—the old me—and think, Wow, she has no idea what's ahead of her.

My entire life, I've always been a planner. I landed a job out of college, moved to New York, and followed a dream I thought was God's plan for my life. It wasn't until I moved back to California and met a man I fell in love with that I realized my life wasn't going to look the way I thought it would.

Brian and my love story began as a blended family. I met my stepchildren when they were nine and eleven, becoming a full-time stepmom in my early twenties. We were married in 2017, and God gifted us a honeymoon baby named Wyatt in 2018. This was our little fuzzy red-headed baby, who had a striking resemblance to Ed Sheeran. I always knew I wanted a second child, and in July 2021, we were blessed with the pregnancy of Weston. I eagerly and happily planned every detail of my future as a boy mom.

I had an uneventful pregnancy. Every scan and checkup showed signs of a perfectly healthy baby boy...until he wasn't. On March 26th, at thirty-nine weeks pregnant, and just four days shy of my due date, I stopped feeling Weston move.

Mom-tuition is a real thing, and I trusted my body that something was wrong. A few hours later, an ultrasound confirmed our worst nightmare. Weston's heart had stopped beating. We will never know why.

That moment and all that followed afterwards was excruciating. My Weston was undeniably beautiful. Seven pounds and one ounce of perfection, with brown curly hair and eyes I will never know the color of.

Those first three months after my loss, my body was in survival mode. The pain was so acute, so physical, and so debilitating. I wanted to get rid of my grief and go back to my older, lighter self. I chased after understanding that never came.

I began feeling God stirring and planting dreams in my heart and mind around nine months after my loss. My questioning of why me, why this, why Weston began evolving to what. What was He trying to teach me about myself and others through these heartbreaking circumstances?

My desperation to try and understand my loss and what happened to me began shifting to what this loss showed me about myself and my purpose here.

I soon realized that God was all I needed when He was all I had. I began clinging to my faith to survive, and as a source of hope that this was not the end of my story. Hope to see my son again. I made the commitment to my faith through baptism on March 26th of 2023, on the one-year mark of my son's passing. The worst day of life is now also shared with a day of hope.

I discovered healing can happen through community. It was through loss support groups I began to no longer feel alone. I found comfort and acceptance amongst people who understood. It was in the Empty Arms Support Group at Saddleback that I met another loss mama, Ashley, who also lost her son. We connected in our pain, but also in our desire to help people.

Together, we joined our talents to create a nonprofit called Gloves for Grief. The product of two women's pain, but also their purpose. This community provides a pathway of resources for grief healing. A focus on the mind, body, and soul.

The boxing gloves are an element of our fitness program; however, they also represent the fight it takes to work through your grief. Fighting for your life and fighting for your comeback. Grief knocked us down, but through the Grace of God, we got back up.

Our desire is to help support as many grievers as possible, no matter the circumstances surrounding your loss. At Gloves for Grief events, we help you punch your pain into purpose.

After fourteen months of intensive grief work, support groups, therapy, and self-care, my grief has progressed.

Progress is the word. I have not "gotten over" my grief. Instead, I have gotten to know my grief. It's part of who I am, and unfortunately, I cannot go back to the person I was before it. My grief is all the love I have for my son, and as long as I live, it will be part of me. Today, I am no longer trying to hide my grief or tears. I am trying to work with my grief, and not against it.

I am developing a community around me of those who "understand" and "get it" without explanation. I am progressing by choosing to honor Weston every chance I can. By no longer shutting down when someone asks me the dreaded "how many kids do you have" question.

I am weaving him into the fabric of our family, even though he's no longer here.

This past year has been a year of indescribable pain. A year of God-given strength. A year of revolutionary change in myself and my family. I could have never predicted that this loss would be part of my story. But I know my story is not over. My grief journey is just beginning. Grief doesn't get easier. We get stronger.

Jodi Rosser – Author of Depth: Growing Through Heartbreak to Strength | Podcaster - *Depth*

What if your greatest heartbreak catapults you to your greatest growth?

This question appears on the back of my book, "Depth: Growing Through Heartbreak to Strength." If I am honest with you, I never set out to be an author. But through my greatest heartbreak, God birthed a ministry through me. Let me take you back to where it all began.

It was the worst day of my life.

Lying alone in my king-sized bed, I tossed and turned. The clock mocked me as the hours read one, then two, then three in the morning. Now, it was 4:00 am, and I hadn't slept a wink. My mind kept replaying the events of the evening over and over in my head. I still couldn't believe that this was the end.

Just hours earlier, I had stood there shocked by what my husband had told me. Like a ton of bricks crashing over my body, the weight of his words was unbearable. Each utterance hurt as if a sword were piercing my heart. I wanted to escape, but I felt completely paralyzed.

As though coming face to face with a mountain lion, my instincts kicked in. My choice was fight or flight. With adrenaline pumping through my body, I had to get away from this giant predatory-sized pain chasing after me. So, I bolted for the stairs.

In the safety of my bedroom, I called my accountability partner, Erin, to share the heartbreaking news. As the phone was ringing, I thought back to the weekly walks Erin and I had been taking together the past several months to purposefully pray for healing in my marriage. I was truly hopeful that God could restore us, but now things looked bleak. When she answered the phone, I sobbed as I shared that my marriage of fifteen years was over.

That night marks the beginning of the hardest year of my life.

The following morning, I woke up and dug through my desk. I remembered hearing a series at my church just months earlier called, "Getting Through What You're Going Through." Pastor Rick Warren had just come back from a hiatus as he grieved the loss of his youngest son. He had just suffered through the greatest heartbreak of his life, and his sermons were some of the most profound and amazing messages he has ever shared. Little did I know then how much I was going to need his wisdom.

Searching for the sermon notes, I read the words I had written on the top of the outline: "God uses pain to fulfill the purposes of your life." Not at all sure how He was going to do that, I kept reading. One of his bullet points said, "I can use my pain to draw closer to God." In the margin, I had scribbled, "You have a choice: you can run to God or run away from God."

There is something about being taken to a place of heartbreak where you have to choose either to run to God with your pain or run away from God in anger. At that moment, I chose to run to the Lord with my pain—every hour, every day, or every minute, if necessary.

I put down the sermon notes, grabbed my pen, and wrote this in my journal: "God, I truly want to grow from my pain. I don't want it to break me. I want it to grow me and help me draw closer to you. Only you can give me strength in this nightmare I am living. Only you can turn my tears into hope. I lay this at your feet. Please take my pain and help me draw closer to you, your power, your strength, your love, and your comfort. Help me to teach my kids to do that too. Help me be an example to them and give me the strength for another day."

I am not going to tell you that life suddenly got easier. I was facing a real storm. The waves kept crashing and the winds kept blowing. I can tell you this: God is faithful. He did give me strength each day, and He can do the same for you. As I cried out to Him each morning, He met me right where I was. Heartbroken. Hurting. Devastated.

He gave me comfort when I felt alone.

He gave me strength to help comfort my kids.

He gave me power to help me get through each day.

Looking back now, I don't know how I got through those first weeks and months. Honestly, I just started with one simple step: inviting God into my pain each day. Sometimes, I breathed a quick prayer, "Help me, God; today, I don't have the strength." Other days, I got up before my kids and journaled. Most often, I clung to a verse that reminded me I was not alone in my grief.

I needed these reminders constantly. Like water to my thirsty soul, I wanted to know that I was not facing this pain alone. On my hard days, it was vital for me to remember that God was walking step by step with me.

God also redeemed my hurt in such a beautiful way. First, it was a blog where I encouraged others by sharing what He was teaching me in the midst of the pain. Then, God continued to bring purpose to the pain through my podcast and my book as I helped others grow deeper in their faith and stronger in their relationships through their unexpected storms.

I believe God wants to bring purpose to your pain, too. So let me ask you again, "What if your greatest heartbreak catapults you to your greatest growth?"

God does not waste one tear.

He is faithful to strengthen you during the storm. He also wants to grow your roots deeper in your faith in a way you never knew possible. And when you are ready to share, He will use your broken story to help another hurting heart.

These are just a few of the many stories where people have used their darkest times and turned them into something positive. Through their circumstances and with faith, they have been able to work through the toughest times of life. They were open to God and His plan to use their life and situations to help themselves heal with hope for the future, while also providing hope and healing to others by sharing their stories and experiences. With God, they have experienced "hope in the darkness," but to do that, they first had to say, "Yes!"

8:28

S

HOPE IN THE DARKNESS

CHAPTER 17
SAYING "YES!"

What's Next?

I could never have made it through the losses in my life without faith and the assurance that I would indeed make it through the loss and that, ultimately, I'd see my babies and family together once again in heaven. For this, I chose to run straight to Jesus and hang on to Him for dear life. I trusted Him to get me through my losses, trusting that through Him, we are saved. My assurance of eternity with my loved ones results from my faith in Him. Without it, I do not believe I could have ever been able to heal healthily or that I would ever have been able to help others heal over the years.

When we are grieving, angry, or afraid and can't see the light at the end of the tunnel, we don't understand that we *can* find hope in the darkness when we walk by faith. We must say, "Yes," in faith; we must trust in God and God's Word to get through our dark times. God has promised us that we will never face the darkness alone, and we need to fully trust in and believe that.

No one will be able to stand against you all the days of your life. As I was with Moses, so I will be with you; I will never leave you nor forsake you.
Joshua 1:5 (NIV)

We must believe we are not alone, even when we can't feel God's presence. He is always with us and wants what is best for us.

Do not fear, for I am with you; do not be dismayed, for
I am your God. I will strengthen you and help you;
I will uphold you with my righteous right hand.
Isaiah 41:10 (NIV)

What an amazing promise! Wouldn't you want to believe this even if you are not strong in your faith? Keep in mind the stories you heard in the previous chapter—amazing stories of survival and testimonies of who got them through it. Please consider the possibility!

God, the Father, is the only one who has the power to overcome the storms of life and the dark times we encounter. God has the power and authority over nature, physical ailments, death, and dying. Through faith in God, we can experience this power as physical, emotional, mental, spiritual, and social healing. So, why wouldn't we say, "Yes!" to Him?

God shows his power over all things in many ways. Here are some passages from the Bible that show how we are assured of that power:

Power Over Nature

In the beginning, God created the heavens and the earth.
Genesis 1:1 (NIV)

The Bible mentions countless ways in which God has power over nature. The Gospels (Matthew 8:26, Mark 4:39, and Luke 8:24) state that Jesus rebuked the wind and silenced the waves, further proof that He can calm the seas in nature and the storms of life.

Power Over Physical Ailments

When Jesus touched her hand, the fever left her. Then she got up and
prepared a meal for him.
Matthew 8:15 (NLT)

*Jesus reached out and touched him. "I am willing," he said. "Be
healed!" And instantly leprosy disappeared.*
Matthew 8:3 (NLT)

*For she thought to herself, "If I can just touch his robe, I will be
healed." Immediately the bleeding stopped, and she could feel in her body
that she had been healed of her terrible condition.*
Mark 5:28-29 (NLT)

*Jesus touched their eyes and said, "Because of your faith, it will
happen." Then their eyes were opened!*
Matthew 9:29 (NLT)

Power Over Death and Dying

Jesus called in a loud voice, "Lazarus, come out!"
*The dead man came out, his hands and feet wrapped with strips of
linen, and a cloth around his face.*
John 11:43 (NIV)

*"For this is how God loved the world: He gave his one and only Son so
that everyone who believes in him will not perish but have eternal life.
God sent his Son into the world not to judge the world, but to save the
world through him.*
*"There is no judgment against anyone who believes in him. But anyone who
does not believe in him has already been judged for not believing in God's
one and only Son. And the judgment is based on this fact: God's light
came into the world, but people loved the darkness more than the light, for
their actions were evil. All who do evil hate the light and refuse to go near
it for fear their sins will be exposed. But those who do what is right come
to the light so others can see that they are doing what God wants."*
John 3:16–21(NLT)

Just as we've seen God's power through the actions of Jesus in so
many other areas, some of the most significant examples involve death.
In Mark 5:35-42, Jesus heals a little girl who died. And the story of

Jesus' resurrection is widely told, showing that Jesus overcame death because God had a plan for his son's life and death, as He does for all of us (Mark 16:1-20).

You may have additional questions about God and the validity of the Bible; if so, consider searching the website "Got Questions" www. gotquestions.org. This site is dedicated to helping people understand God, Scripture, salvation, and many other spiritual topics. All answers on this site are from trained Christian, Protestant, Evangelical, and nondenominational professionals, whose contributions have been reviewed for biblical and theological accuracy. It is not their purpose to make you agree with them but rather to point you to what the Bible says concerning your questions.

The Bible gives many examples of God's power. God is not a genie who will grant all our wishes, but if we are open to His power and plan for our life, we can begin to make sense of things and gain peace and understanding as to why things happen as they do.

Inevitably, people who have situations similar to some you've had will cross your path, or perhaps at least situations you can identify with as a result of your own experiences in times of darkness. I am confident that God does not and will never waste your pain. He promises He will use *all* things for good for those who love Him, so the answer to His prompting and the situations He allows must be "Yes."

Say "Yes" to God's comfort. He is the source for healing our hearts and hurts so that we can help others heal. We are helped every time we can help someone else through their pain, and we are blessed by being a blessing to others. The following is one of my favorite verses—and one I have tried to put into practice throughout my life:

> *"What a wonderful God we have—He is the Father of our Lord Jesus Christ, the source of every mercy, and the one who so wonderfully comforts and strengthens us in our hardships and trials. And why does he do this? So that when others are troubled, needing our sympathy and encouragement, we can pass on to them this same help and comfort God has given us."*
> *2 Corinthians 1:3–4 (TLB)*

Say "Yes" to God, and He will use your hurts and deepest pain to help others. Experience the fruits of the Spirit—love, joy, peace, patience, kindness, goodness, faithfulness, gentleness, and self-control—byproducts of true faith in Him and the essence of who God is. Say "yes" to God's forgiveness, grace, comfort, wisdom, guidance, and His love.

Say "Yes" to God and see how He will heal and turn your darkness into hope and light for others to see. Be open to Him and His healing power and to finding your purpose in and through your times of trials, difficulties, and darkness. Say "Yes" to renewed faith and hope and willingness to share your light and hope in the lives of others. God's plans and purposes for your life are far greater than you could ever imagine, so ask Him to come into your life and show you. We may not fully understand everything as it's happened (or is still happening), but the Bible shows us that faith is vital to gaining understanding.

Walk by faith and not by sight.
2 Corinthians 5:7 (ESV)

I'm confident in knowing that our babies and family members are in heaven, just as I'm secure in the knowledge that I will be with them again someday. Seeing how God has turned our losses into something very big is a blessing, and I know in my heart that involvement in helping others through loss is my purpose. The meaning of Matthew's name is "Gift from God." He was indeed a gift from God, no matter how long he was here. Those we have loved who are no longer here on earth can touch lives daily by the hope others can receive through us as a reflection of God.

For those in the darkness right now, I hope and pray that you will consider this verse and say "Yes." Trust Him to work in your life!

Delight yourself in the Lord and He will give you the desires of your
heart. Commit your way to the Lord; trust in Him and He will do this."
Psalm 37:4,5 (ESV)

Does this mean God will give us everything we want, like a vending machine? No, to delight in the Lord means that we seek to align our hearts with God and His ways. As we grow closer to God and align with Him, our desires will begin to parallel His, and the desires of our hearts will be fulfilled. Seek Him for peace and fulfillment. It can be difficult to consider delight in anything during dark times, but if you can trust that God is on your side and know He wants the best for you, the burden of darkness will be lightened.

I have been open to God's healing and direction in my life, which has been a huge blessing that has extended into the lives of others. I know that everything I have experienced has been according to His plan for my life, although I may not have realized it at the time (in fact, I often thought, "How can this be God's plan?" or "I don't like this plan!").

Are there things I wish I didn't have to go through? Absolutely! But in looking back over my life, I can see more and more how God works "good" in *all* things (just as Romans 8:28 says!)

> *And we know that in __all__ things, God works for the good of those who love him, who have been called according to his purpose.*
> *Romans 8:28 (NIV)*

God is in control, and His plan is good. We all experience darkness in our lives; it is up to us to say *"Yes"* to Him for His healing and hope through the heartbreaks of life.

As I shared in Chapter 1, God led me to write this book. My goal was to help you find purpose, healing, renewed faith, hope, and light in times of heartbreaks, difficulties, and darkness. I hope and pray that you have gained some of these things through reading this book and that you have learned some things about yourself and others through this journey. I hope this book helps you strengthen your faith and change your perspective on what you have been through; perhaps you will even use what you have learned here to help others. And ultimately, I hope this book enables you to find love, faith, peace, healing, and **Hope in the Darkness**.

ENDNOTES

1   Rick Warren is the founder of Saddleback Church in Southern California and author of best selling book "The Purpose Driven Life". Saddleback church is one of the largest churches in the country.

2   Emotional Acceptance: Why Feeling Bad is Good | Psychology Today

3   Emotional Avoidance in PTSD | Verywell Mind Matthew Tull, PHD August 29, 2022

4   Elisabeth Kubler-Ross, On Death and Dying (New York, NY: Scibner, 1969)

5   David Kessler, Finding Meaning: The Sixth Stage of Grief (New York, NY: Simon & Schuster, 2019)

6   *Harvard Business Review*, Kessler applied the five stages of grief to our responses to Covid 19

7   Harold S. Kushner, *When Bad Things Happen to Good People* (Avon, 1983)

8   CS Lewis, *A Grief Observed*, (Harper One, 2015)

9   Ph.D. Kenneth C. Haugk, *Don't Sing Songs to a Heavy Heart*, (Stephen Ministries, 2004)

10 Jerry L. Sittser, *A Grace Disguised: How the Soul Grows Through Loss (Grand Rapids, MI*: Zondervan, 2021)

11 Patrice Karst, *The Invisible String*, (Little, Brown Books for Young Readers, 2023)

12 Tiffany Papageorge, *My Yellow Balloon*, (Minoan Moon, 2014)

13 LeVar Burton & Susan Schaefer Bernardo, The Rhino Who Swallowed a Storm, (Inner Flower Child Books, 2020)

14 Hospice Foundation of America 800-854-3402 www.hospicefoundation.org

15 For King and Country "Hope is What We Crave" CRAVE 2012

16 Steven Curtis Chapman "With Hope" SPEECHLESS Sparrow Records 1999

17 The Serenity Prayer, written by the theologian-philosopher Reinhold Niebuhr.

18 Science Direct Journal Psychosomatic Research Vol. 66, Issue 1 | Gratitude influences sleep

19 StarTribune The Good Life | Minnesota researchers uncover the power of gratitude May 6, 2020

20 Harvard Health Publishing | Exercise is an all-natural treatment to fight depression February 2, 2021

21 The Mayo Clinic | Diseases & Conditions; and Tri-City Medical Center | 5 Ways the Sun Impacts Your Mental and Physical Health